SCHUBERT'S VARIATIONS

A PAGE FROM SCHUBERT'S MANUSCRIPT OF THE VARIATIONS ON A FRENCH AIR, OP. 10 (see p. 33).

SCHUBERT'S VARIATIONS

BY

MAURICE J. E. BROWN

LONDON
MACMILLAN & CO LTD
NEW YORK · ST MARTIN'S PRESS
1954

MACMILLAN AND COMPANY LIMITED

London Bombay Calcutta Madras Melbourne

THE MACMILLAN COMPANY OF CANADA LIMITED

Toronto

ST MARTIN'S PRESS INC

New York

PRINTED IN GREAT BRITAIN

Among the characteristics of a living art is its capacity for extravagance: that is to say, not only its ability to produce lavishly at a great many levels of taste, but also its readiness to be generous, to throw off just for the fun of it the unnecessary incident or decoration.

DILYS POWELL

To
ERIC BLOM

ACKNOWLEDGEMENTS

My sincere thanks are due to Professor Gerald Abraham and to Dr. Otto Erich Deutsch, both of whom read this study of Schubert's variations in manuscript and made many suggestions which led to its improvement and its enrichment. I am also grateful to Dr. Deutsch who has continued to impart to me information on Schubertian manuscripts and matters which have come to his knowledge since the publication of his thematic catalogue of the composer's works. Where, therefore, factual details in this book differ from those in that catalogue they may be taken as deriving from Dr. Deutsch and as being authentic. The late William McNaught kindly gave me the benefit of his sound judgement in several disputable points, particularly where the Schubert and Beethoven spheres momentarily intersect.

I am grateful to Dr. Harold T. Hyman, of New York, who readily gave me permission to reproduce, as a frontispiece, a page from the fragmentary manuscript of Schubert's Op. 10, in his possession.

All extracts from Schubert's own letters have been freshly translated, but quotations from other contemporary documents —advertisements, reviews and so forth—have been taken from 'Schubert: a documentary biography' by O. E. Deutsch. This has been done with the kind permission of the publishers of that book, J. M. Dent & Sons, Ltd.

CONTENTS

ILLUSTRATIONS

CONTENTS

I

SCHUBERT AND VARIATION FORM

Schubert's quality as a composer of variations is assessed mainly on two popular sets, each of them based on an appealing tune, and each constituting a supplementary movement in the work to which it belongs. These variations consist largely of decorations of the subject-melody—mostly attractive, but sometimes tiresome and occasionally trivial: indeed the two movements might almost be subtitled *Air* or *Thème Varié*. The title was used for a purely melodic type of variation very common in Schubert's day, a shallow and showy manifestation of the old and honourable variation form; thousands of these mechanical treatments of popular melodies were perpetrated in the early nineteenth century, Karl Czerny, among others, being responsible for nearly five hundred sets, including, incidentally, a treatment of one of Schubert's own melodies, the celebrated 'Trauerwalzer' (Op. 9: no. 2). As we shall see, Schubert is not always immune from this tendency of his own times to a lighter manner with variation technique.

His work in variation form is accordingly judged, and there are some grounds for such a verdict, to be an inconsiderable part of his output, devoted largely to the melodic aspect of his theme, and insufficiently to the harmonic, rhythmic and contrapuntal implications: by his refusal to adopt the more comprehensive approach, so runs the verdict, he produces results much less attractive to the average informed music-lover. It is arguable in the cases mentioned, the variations on the song *Die Forelle*, which gives the Pianoforte Quintet, Op. 114, its name, and those on a theme from

Die Freunde von Salamanka in the Octet, Op. 166, that the self-sufficient lyricism of the two themes makes them unsuitable variation subjects; and that neither possesses any peculiarities of harmony, of tonal contrasts, or of rhythmic subtlety. This is to say, in other words, that Schubert cannot be blamed for finding none of these materials: his desire in both cases was to present a likeable melody in a number of different guises, and not to treat his theme as a character revealing growth and development, as we feel to be the case even in comparable Beethoven movements, in the slow movement of the 'Kreutzer' Sonata, for instance. Even Schubert's variations on *Death and the Maiden,* while admitted to be of magnificent quality, are briefly dismissed as of the ornamental or 'figured' type, and do not affect the prevailing attitude towards his work in variation form.

Nevertheless, this judgement on Schubert, as a writer of variations, is not broad-based enough to be altogether sound, and it is the purpose of this essay to attempt a reasonable modification of the generally held opinion upon his variations, and, by considering *all* his work in this sphere instead of the most obvious, not only to modify opinion but to draw attention also to many neglected but worthy compositions.

Before leaving the two sets of variations, those in the Pianoforte Quintet and those in the Octet, until a further consideration later, one point may be made. It will be obvious to any listener or student that, perfunctory, decorative and naïve though they sometimes are, there is in both sets a distinct climax: in the first, dramatic and powerful, in the second, complex and ornate. For all their intentionally popular appeal these movements are shapely, they grow in complexity (true, a somewhat mechanically organised growth), they proceed slowly but deliberately from the lyrical to the dramatic, and then—for Schubert is always at his best in this

—the drama quickly subsides to a poetical and lyrical close. In some ways vulnerable to attack as examples of variation-form these two movements yet possess that inner logic which is the true meaning of 'Form', together with a core of excellence which redeems the whole.

The words 'vulnerable to attack as examples of variation-form' need clarifying. The establishment of variation form occurred earlier in the history of music than that of any other persistent modern form. A primitive origin may have lain in the attempts of performers to give interest to the repeated stanzas of songs and dances by introducing changes that would not detract from the essential structure of the melody concerned but would provide relief to the ear. The art of transcribing 'chansons' and the like for keyboard gave rise to the artistic, and recorded, genesis of variation form: a series of different transcriptions—and we have the beginnings of a set of variations, and such variations remained for a long time a purely keyboard form. Accordingly, from the earliest recorded examples of variation cycles—the lute variations of early sixteenth century Spain[1]—up to those of the baroque period the form is concerned chiefly with the varied presentation of a melody—of folk-song, plainsong, chorale and dance-theme, and later of operatic airs. From Byrd and Farnaby to Buxtehude there was this concentration of the composer's craft upon the background or superstructure of his chosen melodic text, which itself underwent little more than rhythmic changes, but which suffered, for all that, submergence.

A contributory factor to the development and enrichment of variations in the classical period was the ripe conclusion of the ancient practice of composing around a given 'tenor'. This

[1] '. . . which do not differ in principle from the towering achievements of Bach, Beethoven and Brahms.' (Alfred Einstein)

occurred in the *basso ostinato* variations of the seventeenth and eighteenth centuries. In this type of 'variations' the sets became continuous, that is, they were not divided into sections according to the length of the theme, and the passacaglias and chaconnes of Pasquin, Couperin and, pre-eminently, Bach revealed new possibilities in the contrapuntal elaboration of motives derived from the theme and built upon the regular procession of the theme itself, usually in the bass. The passacaglia also showed the possibility of an organised approach to a climax of musical interest within a form which did not inherently suggest one.

No clearer record of the great stylistic change in the music of the eighteenth century exists than in the variations of that period: we have only to compare the 'Goldberg' Variations of Bach with the 'Variations in F minor' of Haydn to read the whole history of that mighty revolution. The melody was no longer a subordinate and almost unchanging component in varied contrapuntal textures, it was now the dominating factor, and its attendant harmonies and its own cadential structure governed the processes of the composer's creative thought. The paradoxical result of this new development in variation technique was that the melody, by emerging from its partnership with associated counterpoints began to lose its contours and individuality by reason of the claims of its other components, and the enormous potentialities of thematic development shown by the rise of sonata form.

The possibilities of melodic variation as seen in the variation sets of the late eighteenth and early nineteenth centuries were manifold. They included the simple filling in by scale and fioratura of the melodic intervals, leaving the general outline obvious to the ear of the listener and certainly to the eye of the reader; but they also included the subtle emergence of almost new themes, when mode, time, rhythm, dynamics, phrasing and mood, singly or in combination, were changed by the mind and hand of an artist. To the possibilities of colour change provided in the keyboard variations of the Renaissance and baroque periods by varied register, we now find added that of different instrumentation, for the rise of chamber music ensembles and the establishment of the modern orchestra occurred during that period and played their parts in the changing styles of variation technique.

The melodic variation might be called the objective approach to the theme. Side by side with it, and, in fact, inherent in the form since its inception, there was the treatment of the non-melodic elements in the theme. This is more difficult to categorise. The harmonic structure, the tonality and the cadential phrasing of the theme were present, but there was great freedom in the choice and development of the material derived from the theme which embodied those elements. It was almost as if the particular composer were showing in miniature how his subject, or motives derived from it, might have appeared in the various classical dance and instrumental forms, in the development section of a sonata-movement, in a fugal stretto, in fact, in any musical form where he was stimulated to his most individual output. This could be called the subjective approach to the theme.

It will be seen how much more attractive to the serious composer and listener are the far broader fields of the 'subjective' type of variation. In Beethoven's hands the results are of such surpassing excellence that no subsequent composer of note has ever returned to the purely melodic type in its simplest aspect: Schubert is the last in the long line of composers who wrote them, but it is a mistake to assume that all his variations are of this type only, and equally mistaken to leave out of account those that are as not being worthwhile. It is only by taking the 'subjective' variation, with its range and freedom, as the true manifestation of variation form,

B   S.V.

and withholding cognizance of the 'objective' type, that we can attack Schubert's treatment of *Die Forelle* and the Octet theme.

For in examining the whole question of variation form, of dividing a composer's work broadly into this type or that, the final word does not rest with approval of variations which transmute every element in the theme, and disregard (to use no stronger word) of those which are concerned with only the melodic element; it rests indeed with the value and vitality of the music alone. It is safe to say that Mozart's variations in the first movement of the Sonata in A major (K. 331) and Schubert's variations on *Die Forelle* will still charm and delight future generations while the dust settles on many sets of earnest and painstaking variations written since 1827, faithfully modelled on Beethoven.

This must be the criterion in examining and judging Schubert's variations: not to regret the fact that he chose, in the main, the now obsolete practice of the *Air varié* rather than Beethoven's methods, but to discover whether his variations are alive; whether they have the poetry and tonal magic of his music in other forms; whether or not they deserve the persistent neglect which is their lot.

No attempt will be made in this survey at the kind of analysis whereby every numbered variation is set down from beginning to end, and the reader informed what is happening in each one of them. The merits of such bald cataloguing are very debatable, and it is, in any case, not the aim of the survey to concentrate on minute points of invention and perhaps, by so doing, miss the broader implications of the music as a whole. The following chapters will seek to trace the growth of Schubert's powers as a composer in this form, to relate the examples of it to the rest of his work, to examine his resource in a none too congenial *genre*, and to achieve by such studies an insight into his creative processes.

Schubert wrote sixteen[1] examples in this form ranging from full-scale work like the Pianoforte Duet, Op. 35, to the short and delicate movement called *Andantino Varié*. These sixteen works embrace almost his entire creative years; the earliest is from 1815, the last belongs to 1827. There are two productive periods, 1824 and 1827, but for the rest the work is 'occasional' (perhaps even commissioned by patrons or requested by friends) and infrequent.

This is not to say that it is irrelevant. While Schubert, it is clear, had no strong leanings to the form, fortuitous circumstances, or his wayward genius, or both, extracted master-work from him even here. And when his imagination was fired then the music he produced bears the imprint of his most typical work—it is Schubertian in the accepted sense. The presence of his characteristic qualities, good or bad, in his variations and their relation to his other work render the study of them not only relevant but essential.

Perhaps the report of a personal experience might be permitted here. To the present writer the most familiar of all Schubert's sets of variations has always been that which constitutes the Impromptu in B flat—an acquaintance that dates from boyhood. As this intimate study of his variations drew to a close he reached, at length, the last of them all, the Impromptu. He came to it with opened eyes and a new understanding. It is in the hope of conveying to the reader something of that fresh vision that he offers this study.

With one exception (the 'Introduction and Variations in B flat', Op. 82: no. 2) the dates of composition of all the variations are

[1] This excludes the single variation which Schubert contributed on the 'Diabelli' waltz, and three sets which are lost (see Appendix).

known[1] and it is proposed to deal with them in the only way which will conform to the ideals of this survey, that is, chronologically. There can be no point in dividing them into instrumental categories since well over half of them are written for the pianoforte and of the rest no two are for the same combination of instruments.

In concluding this general introduction one fact may be stressed. As we proceed from the first to the last work there will be found 'no regular scale of gradual improvement' as Edmond Malone said, in like circumstances, of the plays of Shakespeare. To the reader who knows his Schubert—the composer who could follow *Der Doppelgänger* with *Die Taubenpost*, or the delightful Symphony no. 5, in B flat, with that slightest of all his works, Symphony no. 6, in C—this will cause no surprise. Opinions as to which is the finest of all the sets may differ, but there can be no doubt that the vintage period is 1824–1825. Before those years there was an irregular growth to maturity, and after them there followed a corresponding decline. This will become clear as the sets are examined in detail.

[1] The enumerations in square brackets are taken from O. E. Deutsch's 'Schubert: a Thematic Catalogue of all his works in chronological order' (London, 1951).

II

SCHUBERT'S VARIATION STYLE

The presence in Schubert's variations of past techniques of variation form is naturally due to his intuitive absorption of them and not to any deliberate imitation on his part of two centuries of production in the form.[1] Of a few of these historical elements he must have been aware from his knowledge of the work of Haydn, Mozart, Weber and Beethoven, and that of figures such as Czerny, Kalkbrenner and Hummel, minor ones to us, but to him, in the contemporary scene, looming much larger.

Schubert's sixteen sets of variations belong to the early nineteenth century; that is, they stand between the orthodox thematic variations of the seventeenth and eighteenth centuries and the unorthodox or 'free' variations of the nineteenth and twentieth centuries. Since it is proposed to examine in this chapter various matters from his variations in the light of future developments in the form it is of interest and profit to record also the few ways in which they derive from and link with the works which preceded them.

The most immediate connection lies in his use of contrasted variations—in the opposite mode to that of the tonic key, or in slower tempos, usually called '. . . *più lento*', rarely *Adagio*. This derives from the conventional 'minore' and '*Adagio*' sections familiar in the work of his predecessors. The eighteenth century practice obtained during the course of the variations something of

---

[1] *Cf.* Richard Capell's comment on Bruckner: 'The past existed in him, as in all true creative artists, at a level rather lower than consciousness'.

9

the contrast of tempos and keys in the movements of a sonata. In his book on Brahms' work in variation form Viktor Luithlen compares the '*Adagio*' variation with the slow movement of a sonata. Schubert intensifies the resemblance by using, as well, 'scherzando' types of variation.

Another traditional factor in Schubert's variation technique is the way in which he progressively intensifies and animates the music of succeeding variations. This, as was pointed out in the previous chapter, was a development noticeable in the chaconnes and passacaglias of the late baroque period; it is a remarkable and familiar feature in Bach's Chaconne in D minor for solo violin. It is manifestly present in the keyboard variations of Mozart (see the finale of the Sonata in D, K. 284) as Paul Mies, in his study of Mozart's variations has pointed out. In Schubert's hands it becomes a conventional procedure in the initial group of variations in each of his sets but he has his own individual methods of departure from it. The chaconne technique may be responsible for another frequent feature in his variations. Many of them are written for pianoforte duet and there is a marked tendency for Schubert to give the theme to the bass in 'Secondo' and to superimpose on it elaborate counterpoints and figuration in 'Primo'. The technique is not, however, confined to the works for pianoforte duet but appears effectively in his chamber music variations on *Der Tod und das Mädchen* and *Die Forelle*.

It is, of course, obvious that in Schubert's choice of these song themes, and others, for variation subjects he was using a device as old as variation form itself (although not in the fact that the songs were his own). Only once did he resort to the popular operatic extract on which to base variations, although the work of Mozart and Beethoven abounds with such examples; for him to base a variation-movement in a chamber music work on a popular opera-

tic aria, as Beethoven did, is unthinkable. What of the occasional
Lied-variation we find in his sets? Is this a survival of, or a reversion to the song or chorale variation of the eighteenth century? It
undoubtedly springs from his irrepressible desire for song-like
forms.

A final historical element present in some of his sets is the
'variation-pair' of the baroque period, that is, a variation followed
by another which is elaborated from it. A slender link, it is true,
since the second one of Schubert's pair, although obviously based
on the first, does not follow immediately after it. But it is a device
the antiquity of which he must have known. Was it due to Salieri's
instruction? One of the noticeable uses of it occurs in the 'Ten
Variations in F major' of 1815 composed while he was still a pupil
of the Italian master, and it seems not unlikely that Salieri oversaw
this particular work, since in the superscription Schubert styles
himself 'Écolier de Salieri'.

The elements in Schubert's variations which point to subsequent developments in the form are of greater interest than those
which derive from the past. The most important of them is found
in those variations of his maturity in which there is a free and
adventurous departure from the basic structure of his theme. Vin-
cent d'Indy, although unaware apparently of Schubert's full originality in this line, calls such a variation 'la variation amplifi-
catrice'. It was an astonishing departure in Schubert's day,
although the slow movement of the Sonata in A minor, Op. 42, as
will be seen, provides an instance of even greater originality. In
these 'variations amplificatrices' Schubert abandons a *strict* al-
legiance to the cadential structure of the text and allows his derived
variation-theme to expand as his imagination dictates. Occasionally, and as remarkably, there occurs a *contraction* of the text with,

in one case, a variation in the set on Hérold's theme, a strikingly effective result. Associated with this amplification, or contraction of the structure of his theme we find an extraordinary range of keys—an impermissible range if we judge by the criteria of previous masters. Even Beethoven in his last quartets and sonatas rarely departs very far from the tonic key of his theme; the theme of the variation-movement of his Op. 127 is in A flat major and the only key departures are to E major and C sharp minor.[1] In the long series of variations in C major on the 'Diabelli' waltz Beethoven abandons the tonic key for only C minor and E flat major. Compare Schubert's key-scheme in the set, Op. 10, which he dedicated to Beethoven, and which was written years before that master's Op. 127: the theme is in E minor, and of the eight variations, four only are in that key, two are in E major, one in C major, and one in C sharp minor. And equally varied schemes occur in other sets.

This free treatment, especially noticeable in the slow movements of the Fantasia in C, Op. 15, and of the Sonata in A minor, Op. 42, points the way to the unorthodox techniques of the nineteenth and early twentieth century, in the work of Franck, d'Indy, Strauss and Delius. It carries its dangers. By writing variations a composer submits to the discipline of his theme; it is obvious from the work of Beethoven and Brahms that their finest and most profound music is produced when a stricter obedience to the text-theme is present. Their craft in that music is the more admirable since the result is so flexible and characteristic. The unlicensed variations of the middle and late nineteenth century have produced very attractive examples, but ones which are fundamentally lighter and in a more popular vein. Unless the disciplinary restraint of the

---

[1] Beethoven's exceptional use of keys in his Op. 34 is an isolated case; it obviously had no influence whatever upon his usual procedures.

strict variation is submitted to, the form is apt to become a loose association of free fantasias on derived motives, motives incidentally, as in Schumann's 'Études Symphoniques', whose connection with the theme is apparent only on paper. The greater depth of feeling which distinguishes the Romantic variation when 'strict' variation form returns is surely obvious in Elgar's 'Enigma' Variations. The personal style and innate desires of the composer are naturally inseparable from his choice between the two alternative methods: with Schubert one feels that the continual discipline of his text-theme is to a certain degree a limiting and confining one. Within the scheme of 'strict variation' episodes he will burst out, as it were, and produce one or two unorthodox variations of the highest poetry or emotional depth; the practice can be seen in the variations of Op. 35, in the *Andantino Varié*, Op. 84, and elsewhere. But these original flights take their value and effect from the strict environment in which they occur and from which comes their stimulus. It is of interest, in this connection, to consider the words of Charles Morgan on sonnet-form: '. . . rule is necessary' he says, 'as the order of Nature is necessary, so that we may be aware of miracles . . . in ruleless art there can be no perceptible variants, no break in the tedium of absolute licence.' For Schubert to create a work consisting entirely of these 'variations amplificatrices', each maintaining the standard and interest of his best efforts—it would be incongruous to his aims and methods.

Finally, in his occasional resort to a sustained and effective, but non-fugal, finale, he foreshadows later practices. These finales are rarely, in his best works, vigorous and powerful, quite the reverse; but they are not merely strict, elaborate treatments of the subject as was usual in his day. Rather do they bring the work to a soft, lingering close.

Most of Schubert's sets of variations are short works; the longest one he wrote comprises the thirteen variations on a theme by his friend Anselm Hüttenbrenner. The rest have numbers ranging from four to eight. There is nothing to compare with Beethoven's sets of over thirty variations, to mention contemporary work only. It is understandable that, working within such compact limits, his method of organising a work in variation form became over the years a standardized practice: the first tentative example is in the 'Variations on a French Air', Op. 10, of 1818. Into the first two or three variations he introduces an increasing complexity of theme or accompaniment by rhythmic or harmonic elaboration; then there follow more adventurous and, it must be confessed, more individual and interesting episodes. The texture is simpler, the music hushed, and bold strokes of harmony or melody or modulation elevate the musical thought and design. In a few cases the conventional opening variations and the bolder ones which succeed them are linked by an interlude consisting of a simple *Lied*-variation where the theme is given a Schubertian, singing quality and appears over simple accompaniment figures. The set then concludes with a final variation of importance, and, in one case, with an independent finale. Towards the end of his career Schubert imitated in some of his last sets, and successfully, a procedure he must have known from various works of Mozart and Beethoven, namely, the rounding off of his piece by a repetition of the theme, or a shortened version of it, at the end of the final variation. He would have known of the examples in the finales of Mozart's String Quartet in D minor (K. 421) and of Beethoven's, Op. 109, to mention two well known movements. His Impromptu in B flat contains a successful use of the procedure.

The first few variations in each of his sets, which always adhere closely to the theme, have none of the interest which obtains in analogous variations of Haydn, Mozart or Beethoven. It has been said that for Schubert the form was a confining one; he allows each bar of his theme to dictate the shape and content of each corresponding bar in these earlier numbers of a set. Sometimes the result can be monotonous in the extreme, as in the Fantasy for violin and pianoforte, Op. 159, where a chromatic cadence in the melody comes over and over again without respite at the appropriate place in the variations. One feels up against a certain *obtuseness* in his method here; with precisely similar work of the older masters, so versatile and inventive, as his models, it is difficult to see why he should so repeatedly aim at the spirit of their work, only to miss even the letter of it. His derived motives are too close to the theme itself and no chance evolution from their treatment, lyric or dramatic, is ever allowed to take wing as it would in the songs of the period. Each is severely cramped into the mould of the original theme. His elaboration of the melody and the harmonic scheme is in complete contrast to the tendency towards simplification of *texture* such as we find in Mozart; and that composer's novelties of rhythmic and thematic change are without heirs in Schubert's similar work. Rather is Schubert's method to adopt Beethoven's sonorities, linear figuration and textural richness, but he cannot achieve the older composer's individual variety of motival derivation.

A most extraordinary factor in Schubert's variation style is the entire absence of scholastic devices in a form which almost demands them; fugato, canon, invertible counterpoint, syncopation, augmentation and the like are conspicuous by their absence, nor is there one example of the use of fugue as a finale. As in other works of his, his favourite device of imitation abounds, and his free and skilful use of it provides examples of counterpoint

as notable as would be called for if he had used the orthodox
forms.

Of Schubert's style in general in the variations one can only
affirm that there is in them the same pervading excellence as in all
his other works; let his formal shortcomings and rhythmic grace-
lessness and monotony receive due castigation: on grounds of
style, that is, the masterly use of music as a language, he is un-
assailable. He used music as a means of lucid communication of
thought as fluently and easily as most of us use speech. Whether
it is in the articulation of his melody, in the unexpected but un-
failingly right and picturesque choice of harmony, in the lay-out
of chords, in the vitality and aptness of accompanying figures, or
in the disposing of his music for its medium, there is no flaw.
Some of those claims are not familiar in connection with his keyboard work in general—but most admirable are the beautifully
apposite and stylish chromaticism of his harmony and its always
perfect disposition in chords. This masterliness, in which Mozart
does not excel him and Beethoven does not approach him, is en-
countered again and again in his song accompaniments, as well as
in the keyboard variations. It cannot be claimed, however, that
the disposition of the music for the player's hands is beyond criticism: but that is a different matter. The preludes and postludes of
his songs, and the varied fabrics of his variations, are full of these
jewels of chromatic harmony and modulatory excursions upon
the firm diatonic basis of his chosen key—see, as merely one example, the choiceness of the prelude to the song *Sei mir gegrüsst*,
whose theme he used, years afterwards, for variations. This use of
delicate and refined chromatic harmony beneath diatonic themes
which do not imply it evokes great depths of tenderness and feeling—the Schubertian pathos so typical of his music; it can readily
be seen in those small and unregarded songs of his formative years

such as *Der Abend, Das Geheimnis* and *Furcht der Geliebten* (all of 1815), so that they are, to the student, more interesting than those made famous by the singers.

What of these variations, if they are considered as the productions of an artist working in Austria, during the dozen years after the Congress of Vienna? Amongst the composers of the Viennese school, that artist was the only one native to the capital. Vienna was to the others their city of adoption; he was its child. The fact has led to a great deal of attempted identification between the atmosphere of early nineteenth century Vienna and the manner and content of Schubert's music—supposedly more marked, in his case, than in that of Haydn, Mozart, Beethoven and so on. The attempt to draw this parallel would be the more convincing were it not always assumed that the qualities germane to the Austrian capital and to the music of its only native composer are always those of gaiety and the carefree heart. Like all creative artists of the front rank Schubert is dyed in the emotional and spiritual colours of his own period and environment, but his most masterful work is free from the accidents of time and place, and stands with the timeless greatness of all the world's supreme music. Thus, we may look upon the variations he wrote for the Hérold theme, for the Impromptu in B flat, and for the Octet, as embodying the spirit—or what is understood by the spirit—of Congress Vienna; but in the finest of his essays—in Opp. 35 and 42 and the variations of the 'Death and the Maiden' quartet—we find nothing of that transient and shallow glitter, dance and sentimentality of the Vienna of his day.

Schubert's variations have not been the object of serious consideration by the scholar, and, with a few exceptions, they are

ignored by the performer. His departures from conventional procedure, which will be dealt with in more detail in subsequent chapters, have been without influence on the work in variation form
produced in the nineteenth century simply because his best examples were unknown to the majority of musicians. The evidence
for this is to be found in the complete absence of recorded references to them, and in the lack of performances; and although
seven of the sixteen sets were published in his lifetime the rareness
of reprinted editions in the nineteenth century speaks for itself.

III

EXPERIMENTAL YEARS: 1815–1818

1. *Andante* from Symphony no. 2, in B flat.
2. Ten Variations in F major.
3. Variations on a theme of Anselm Hüttenbrenner.
4. Eight Variations on a French Air, Op. 10.
5. Introduction, variations and finale in B flat, Op. 82: no. 2.

Schubert's first five sets of variations, written in his youth, form a heterogeneous collection. Apart from the unadventurous choice of medium, since all but one were written for the pianoforte, they were experimental essays in which he tested various schemes and devices, and by trial and error sought to find a congenial procedure in an uncongenial form. The themes themselves are indicative of this testing process: some are original, some are borrowed from others; some are extremely simple, some are long and complex; all are in duple or quadruple time, and this preference remains noticeably in evidence throughout his life. The number of variations in each set ranges from four to thirteen; the latter quantity is exceptional—he was usually content in later years, or had exhausted his resources, with eight, or fewer variations.

The one variation-movement not for the pianoforte is, surprisingly, for orchestra; it is his first extant example of the form (the two earlier sets, both lost, were for pianoforte) and he never used so ambitious a medium again. The movement is simple to bareness. It is also the only one of these youthful essays which forms part of a larger work; the other four are all independent pieces, and the conclusion is clear, that variation-form as a basis for a sonata-movement was not a first choice of the composer—only three examples, or possibly four (see Op. 84: no. 1), of such a choice occur in his very numerous works in classical 'four-movement' structure.

The long break between the 'Ten Variations in F major', composed in February, 1815, and the variations on a theme of Anselm Hüttenbrenner of August, 1817, was due perhaps to his intense concentration on songs and operas in those months. The designation of the period as 'long' is a relative use of the term: in Schubert's short, intense creative life two and a half years is a considerable gap. We shall find similar breaks in the sequence of variations in the next five years, but in those five there were also breaks in the sequence of chamber and orchestral works, and that is more regrettable.

The most strikingly experimental of all five sets is the second, the set in F major; there is nothing in his later work, even in the masterpieces of 1824–1826, to compare with its ranging variety. The gradual establishment of his method with the form, which was eventually to become an almost conventionalized treatment, is first found in Op. 10, the variations on a French Air, written in the summer of 1818.

All the sets, except the first orchestral movement, were published by various firms, in Vienna and Hamburg, during the nineteenth century; in fact, the *Andante* from his second symphony was the only set of variations which remained for the 'Gesamtausgabe' to publish for the first time.

1. *Andante* FROM SYMPHONY NO. 2, in B FLAT   [D.125]
   Small Orchestra.   January, 1815

Several points of interest attach to this movement, the first extant set of variations by Schubert which we possess. Most of these points, it must be admitted, are external to the work itself for the music is slight and innocuous. The slenderness of this *Andante* is surprising since the other three movements of the symphony are of such interest that, among the six symphonies of Schubert's youth, this one ranks second in importance only to No. 5, also in B flat, composed in the following year. Symphony no. 2 was not published until 1884, in Breitkopf and Haertel's 'Gesamtausgabe'; the manuscript is now in the possession of the Vienna *Gesellschaft der Musikfreunde*. England claims the honour of having first performed the work in public; it was given at the Crystal Palace on 20 October 1877, conducted by August Manns.

The choice of variation-form for his slow movement, with an original theme for its basis, was in the nature of an experiment on Schubert's part: he never repeated it in his symphonies, and only once more—ten years later, in the Sonata in A minor, Op. 42— do we find another instance of the practice.

This early use of the form brings with it no innovations; the composer follows, as young composers do, the outward conventionalities of the form, and, after coping with them, he has no energy left to lavish on ardent invention or bold novelty. The fashion of his day, to ensure correspondence between theme and variation, is slavishly followed, and given the first bar of each of his variations in this movement one could fairly safely predict the rest of it.

In the symphonic *Andante* the theme is seventeen bars long: an eight bar phrase answered by one of nine bars. All the variations are identically similar to this in construction. The brief coda, departing from this pattern, brings a relief to the ear out of all proportion to its worth.

The Haydnesque theme is naïve, charming and not without formal merit; it has an obvious kinship with the theme in *Die*

c   s.v.

Freunde von Salamanka which forms the basis of the variations in the Octet. The two themes were, in fact, composed within a few months of each other.

Ex. 1

The grace notes in bar 6 (and again in bar 16) would stamp the work as belonging to 1814–1816 without external evidence. They are a feature of Schubert's style in that period, a non-integrated superfluity which is unwelcome; this particular ornament in his hands is apt to lend a certain perkiness to his utterance. In the opening movement of his first sonata, in E major, which must have been written very soon after these variations, grace notes smother the delicate second subject with gay triviality like an Adam ceiling decked with paper chains.

The second section of the theme opens with a sequence which deserves a comment; it is Schubert's first important use of a harmonic progression by which a perfect cadence in the tonic key is approached by one in the supertonic. Although the progression was, of course, common coin in the musical currency of his age, he is to do some magical things with it during the next dozen years. It appears in the theme (bars 9–12) as

Ex. 2

To Schubert it must have been a very satisfying association of cadences—as indeed it is: his songs show many aspects of it, probably because its couplet form matched to a nicety corresponding literary devices. Possibly the loveliest and most poignant phrase

in the whole of Schubert is the Neapolitan modification of this cadence to be found in the 1826 song *Im Frühling*[1] where the poet contrasts departing love with abiding sorrow—'Die Lieb' und ach! das Leid'.

The theme of the symphonic movement is announced by the strings of the orchestra; there follow five variations. The first two and the fifth merely display a slightly richer accompaniment to the theme, which is almost untouched; the third uses the harmonic scheme only. The orchestration throughout is of a remarkable clarity, and has, at the same time, a cool, pastel quality. In so far as it is possible to analyse this quality, it is due to the sparing use of violas, cellos and basses for the purpose of accompaniment. When they are not engaged with the theme or its derivatives, they are either given light, pizzicato touches or are silent altogether; in vars. I and III the woodwind counterpoints are accompanied by the violins alone, with occasional support from the two horns, pianissimo. Similar effects were used in the first movement.

The best and most spacious of the variations is the fourth, in C minor. Moreover, in the light of subsequent work, it takes on an added interest, for, a few months later, Schubert used the form if not the mood of these arching triplets in the postlude of his setting of Klärchen's song from Goethe's 'Egmont', a postlude which itself wonderfully sums up the music of the whole song.

It is impossible to resist drawing attention to the Trio section of the *Menuetto* which follows the *Andante*. Here Schubert was surely writing a sixth variation, and a pleasant one at that:

Ex. 3

[1] This song might almost be considered as an example of Schubert's variations: see Richard Capell's remarks in his book 'Schubert's Songs', p. 217.

Reference to the closing bars of this Trio, and to those of the *Andante* theme, will reveal a close connection, as if to show that Schubert's mind was still working, subconsciously, on the possibilities of his variation-theme.

2. Ten Variations in F major   [D.156]

Pianoforte Solo.   February, 1815

Shortly after the completion of the variations in his second symphony, before even the finale of the symphony was written, Schubert composed a set of ten variations, on an original theme, for the pianoforte. The manuscript was sold by his brother, Ferdinand, early in 1830, to Diabelli & Co., of Vienna, but they never published the work. It went eventually to another Viennese firm, Weinberger & Hofbauer, who published it in 1887. From them the manuscript passed to the collector Charles Malherbe, and from him, finally, to the Library of the Conservatoire de Paris. It consists of six folios, and (as if by some uncanny premonition of its ultimate destination!) it was inscribed by Schubert:[1]

'X variations pour le Fortepiano composés par Francois Schubert, Ecolier de Salieri, premier Maitre de la Chapelle imperiale et royale de Vienne. 1815.'

At the end of the manuscript the composer wrote 'Am 15. Februar 1815. Fine'.

The work is more significant than its predecessor in the form, and since it pre-dates by some two years the finest of the early sonatas, it can be considered as his first work of importance for the pianoforte. It is true that similar limitations of design are present: in each variation save the last, which is extended to serve the purpose of a finale, there is the same obsequious bending of the motival patterns to the dictates of the theme as was observed in

[1] His faulty French has been left as he wrote it.

the symphonic movement. There is no question that Schubert was unable to comprehend at this early stage in his career the necessity for inventing subsidiary themes for his variations which, although based upon his subject, have yet a distinction and hall-mark of their own: typical of themselves and of their composer. There is all the difference in the world between the variation themes which Mozart derives from his subject in the first movement of the A major Pianoforte Sonata (K.331) and Schubert's mere paraphrases of the melody in F major which he provides for each of his ten variations. Nor is his treatment so expert, within the confines of the theme, as to compensate for this meagreness of invention.

To take one example only: in the fourth variation the music has a quality both grave and delicate:

Ex. 4

Ideas of this kind produce the poetical miniatures in his songs of the same year (1815), as in *An die Sonne* (Baumberg) or *Nacht-gesang* (Kosegarten); but this variation pursues its predestined course.

Nevertheless, circumscribed as it is, the piece has much to commend it. There is considerable variety of both technical and emotional values, a sense of climax, a consistently interesting keyboard style, and an effective finish. It would be a good choice for the pianist who wished to play a shorter Schubert work, and yet to avoid the over-played Impromptus and 'Moments Musicaux'.

The twenty-one bars of the theme (marked originally by

Schubert *Andante Molto*) display to perfection his flexible handling of phrase-balance, his constant care to avoid 'four-square' rhythms. Beneath the spontaneous flow of notes his calculating hand is at work: in the way the phrase which brings section 1 to a close in the dominant is skilfully and smoothly used for the final bars in the tonic key; in the delaying of the caesura (bars 13 and 14) by an echoing device borrowed from his song-writing. From the same source came the art by which the return to the opening phrase is made—the music seeming to take breath. There is once more, in this theme, the favourite 'supertonic-tonic' progression used to initiate section 2 as was remarked upon in the variation-theme of the second symphony. Every time this progression occurs in the series of variations its melodic superiority and the imaginative treatment it gets heighten the value of the music; the result is that each variation, however modest its beginning, improves considerably as it goes on. The accompaniment suggests a string quartet. It is strange to have to admit here that Schubert's craft is more admirable than his melody, but it is so; the theme is a rather unenterprising one, and this is all the more regrettable since it so completely dominates its progeny of variations.

Considered as a whole the work is possibly of more importance in the development of Schubert's keyboard style than for its own specific worth; most of his later technical mannerisms make their first appearance, and not merely in embryo. Three may be mentioned:

(1) There is the use of repeated chords in which one or the other of the component parts wavers between concord and discord to give an almost contrapuntal interest to the fundamental harmony: the device is to appear at its most mature in the 'Impromptu in C minor', Op. 90: no. 1; it is present in vars. II and V of this work in F major.

(2) There are the scales which ascend and descend over rhythmic chords as in vars. III and X: this is an elaboration very characteristic of his early fantasias, his impromptus, and all his variations for keyboard, designed to give them brilliance and pianism, but in fact not too wisely conceived for either purpose. We shall meet it again at its most obvious in the variations of Op. 15 and of the Impromptu in B flat.

(3) There is the bass formed on a pattern of moving unisons or octaves which stalk below a straightforward version of the melody, and which can be seen in var. VI.

It is worthy of study to discover how the first two of these features are used to obtain 'variation-pairs' and so turned to practical use in securing unity between variation and variation. The moving parts in the chords of var. V provide the *scherzando* theme of var. VII; the semiquaver octaves in the bass of var. VI are modified into a dotted semiquaver rhythm for the 'Hungarian Dance' theme in var. VIII.

The fourth variation suggested material for a short *Écossaise* in D minor [D.158] written a few days afterwards:

Ex. 5

The fact is mentioned here, in passing, to draw brief attention to an unexplored tract in Schubertian studies, an investigation of the part played in his creative development by his dance music, particularly in the establishment of his instrumental rhythms, style and harmony, and the reciprocal benefitting of each group by the other.

A technical matter of importance in Schubert's style is the way in which he will increase the interest and importance of descant-like figures instead of allowing them to fade out in the course of the passage as lesser composers will; this is a sure instance of the hidden influence of Beethoven upon his procedures in these early years, and it can be seen in a tentative fashion in var. IX of this set. A further Beethoven feature is present in the use of the continuous trill in the same variation; its appearance is a little self-conscious and Schubert rarely used it again to any marked extent, but the way in which he afterwards made so personal a use of the feature can be seen in the first movement of his posthumous Sonata in B flat, and in the String Quintet in C major. So, too, the use of cadenzas in vars. VII and X is more in the manner of Mozart and Beethoven than in his own. The heart of the work, var. IV, reveals the true Schubertian poetry, and nothing is finer in the whole series than his treatment here of the cadential progression from bars 10 and 11 of his theme.

3. VARIATIONS ON A THEME BY ANSELM HÜTTENBRENNER [D.576]

Pianoforte Solo.   August, 1817

Schubert made the acquaintance of Anselm Hüttenbrenner when they were both pupils of Salieri. Hüttenbrenner came from Graz, and adopted music as a career after abandoning a legal one. He was the eldest son of affluent parents, and two of his younger brothers, Josef and Heinrich, also became acquaintances of Schubert. Josef, who came to Vienna in 1818, acted as an unofficial and unpaid secretary to Schubert in the early 1820's, and for a time was his devoted admirer.

Of all Schubert's acquaintances, the brothers Anselm and Josef become, on deeper examination, more and more deserving of contempt. One finds oneself eyeing them askance. The attitude of mid-nineteenth century Schubertian biographers and writers of memoirs towards the two men, expressed while they were still living, is understandably enough guarded and without censure. Their estimation of the two men's characters was accepted by later writers and a false picture of the Hüttenbrenners was incorporated into the Schubertian background. The gradual bringing to light of their own letters and other authentic information about them have, however, changed that picture. What Anselm, himself a composer, really felt as the passing of time added to Schubert's renown is fairly obvious from his behaviour in later years. He returned to Graz in 1818, and, except for a brief period in Vienna, that town became the centre of his activities. When, in September, 1827, Schubert visited Graz as the guest of the charming and accomplished Marie Pachler, there must have been in Anslem's mind something of the feelings of the provincial composer towards his fellow from the capital, from the centre of musical affairs. Years after Schubert's death Josef's admiration of him was soured by a jealous preference for his brother's, Anselm's, music. In those years neither brother showed up particularly well as a possessor of valuable Schubertian MSS. This is not the place to probe into the matter but it remains one of the more interesting ancillary studies in Schubert.

The theme which forms the basis of these variations comes from the *Andantino* of Anselm Hüttenbrenner's String Quartet no. 1, in E major, published by Steiner & Co. of Vienna, in 1817. The attraction of the *Andantino* for Schubert clearly lies in its affinity with his well loved Beethoven movement, the *Allegretto* from that composer's seventh symphony. The powerful impression made by that movement can be felt almost to the end of Schubert's career, and many times in this study of his variations reference will have to be made to the results of that impression. The rhythmic sense of the *Allegretto* is not absent from the previous set of variations. Hüttenbrenner's theme is a very mild paraphrase of it.

Schubert, in August 1817, composed thirteen variations on the theme. His work was published fifty years afterwards by Diabelli's successor, C. A. Spina, who dedicated it to Anselm Hütten-brenner. It is possible, of course, that Schubert intended such a dedication, although there is no record of it on the manuscript which is still extant and in the possession of the Vienna City Library. The set is less interesting than that in F major of 1815. The variations are smoother, more controlled, more graceful, but they lack the vigour, the brilliance, the variety, and even the healthy vulgarity of the preceding series. Each variation adheres closely to the theme in the usual manner of those years, but this time to the adherence is also added something of deference. The work provides the only example of Schubert's writing variations on a theme by a personal friend, and his handling of it suggests a certain delicacy, as though he feared to indulge in the customary Schubertian adventurousness.[1] Little is done except to add scale-like decorations above or below the theme, in unisons or octaves; occasional chromatic passing-notes and chords are introduced, but they are never allowed to obscure the main lines of the melody. The monotony is not alleviated by change of key, time-signature or tempo: all the variations, except the last, are in 2/4 time, and no fewer than nine are in A minor.

Whether the composer kept in mind throughout his work that he was dealing with a theme from a string quartet, or whether that was an unconscious factor, the style unmistakably derives from that medium. Although there is some truth in the adverse criticism which has been made from time to time that Schubert's music for the pianoforte suggests reduction from another medium, it cannot

---

[1] His deference to his friend's music was not reciprocated. In 1821 Anselm actually published in Vienna a set of waltzes based on the *Erlking*, an act of vandalism which drew even from Schubert a mild protest.

be applied too generally. But these 'Hüttenbrenner' variations
would justify it. Var. V not only suggests string quartet writing:
it actually foretells the style of the variations which he was to
write later on for the 'Death and the Maiden' theme:

Ex. 6

On the other hand the only 'pianistic' variation in the set, the
tenth, is most gratefully so, using a figuration of broken chords
with which to embellish the theme. We have here almost the only
indication that the work belongs to 1817, the year of Schubert's
devotion to the pianoforte, as remarkable in its way as the song-
years, 1815 and 1816. Perhaps not the only indication, since in the
previous variation, no. IX, the adoption of the major key sets the
music moving freely and melodiously, and the slow movement of
the Sonata in E minor (June 1817) is recalled. Both pieces, the
sonata movement and the ninth variation, contain early examples
of his use of undulating arpeggios as an accompaniment, arpeggios
which fall from the equal notes of his theme in a manner which
derives from his songs (cf. the E major section of *Die Erwartung*
1815). It is a feature which persists throughout his pianoforte
writing; its finest use is found in the lilting first variation of the
Impromptu in B flat (1827).

The variety and interest which scholastic devices could have
given to these variations on so stolid a theme are eschewed completely by the composer. For a moment, at the beginning of var.
XI canon is suggested, but it is given up at once in favour of
homophonic texture.

The final variation, no. XIII, is extended beyond the alloted sixteen bars, and its hammering rhythms and bold shifts (e.g. C sharp minor to C major) point to the real Schubert. With an obvious sense of relief he let himself go in this finale, for it concludes a work in which he repressed almost all that was typical of his genius.

4. EIGHT VARIATIONS ON A FRENCH AIR IN E MINOR, OP. 10.
[D.624]

Pianoforte Duet.   July 1818

These variations for pianoforte duet on a French song were composed by Schubert during his stay at Zseliz in the summer of 1818 when he acted in the capacity of music teacher to the children of Count Esterházy. The castle of Zseliz, in Hungary, was the summer residence of the Esterházy family; they spent the winter in Vienna. Schubert's chief duty was to instruct the two daughters of the Count, Marie and Caroline, who both played the pianoforte, and who, in 1818, were respectively 16 and 13 years old. This was the first of two occasions on which Schubert visited Zseliz, the second occurring six years later. Both periods were productive, for obvious reasons, of pianoforte duets, and there is a curious parallelism between the two groups of duets: amongst other works a sonata and a set of variations were composed on each occasion. 1818 gave rise to the Sonata for four hands in B flat, Op. 30, and the variations under consideration; 1824 to the Sonata for four hands in C major, Op. 140 (called the 'Grand Duo'), and the 'Variations on an original theme' in A flat, Op. 35.

The French song is a Romance entitled 'Le bon Chevalier', a setting of words beginning 'Reposez-vous, bon Chevalier...' and said to be the work of Queen Hortense of Holland (1783–1837). It is no. 5 of the 'Romances mises en musique par S.M.L.R.H.' (that is, Sa Majesté la Reine Hortense); the actual composer is in all probability the celebrated flautist Louis Drouet. There was a volume of these airs at Zseliz (editions: Paris, 1813 and Leipzig, 1817) and this particular one may have been brought to Schubert's notice because it was a favourite with the Esterházy family. He must, in any event, have been aware of the many sets of variations which Mozart had composed on French airs.

A manuscript sketch of Schubert's, now in the Isham Memorial Library, Harvard University,[1] for some of the polonaises in Op. 75, has only recently emerged from obscurity; on it the French air appears as if written down from a first hearing: there are trifling differences between it and the authentic version. Incidentally, this manuscript sketch, dated 'July 1818', gives us indications of the date and place of composition of the earliest of these polonaises, indications which hitherto were quite unknown.

The variations were published on 19 April 1822 by Diabelli as Schubert's Op. 10 and dedicated to Beethoven 'by his admirer and worshipper, Franz Schubert' ('von seinem Verehrer und Bewunderer'). The manuscript survives in a fragmentary state, part of it (the theme, var. I and part of var. II) in private possession in Vienna, another part (var. III and parts of var. II and var. IV) in the Sibley Music Library, Rochester University, New York, and a third portion in private possession in New York. The four-stave structure of the manuscript, without any indication of instrumentation, led to the assumption that this third portion was part of an unpublished Pianoforte Trio,[2] but it consists, in fact, of a substantial section (bars 38–63) of the last variation (no. VIII).

The story of the sequel to the publication may be one of those highly improbable anecdotes about Schubert which sprang up so

----

[1] In the bequest of Otto Dresel.

[2] See O. E. Deutsch's 'Schubert: a thematic catalogue', p. 12, note 1. One page of the fragment is reproduced in the frontispiece.

profusely in the mid-nineteenth century, and which for decades
have cluttered up the Schubertian biographies and falsified the
composer's character, temperament and procedure: the blank
pages of his life have invited too many scribblers. He is said to
have called on Beethoven to present a copy of the variations in
person. Two versions of what happened, quite irreconcilable one
with the other, tempt us to believe neither. Anton Schindler
stated that Beethoven discomfitted Schubert by pointing out an
elementary fault in the music, Josef Hüttenbrenner that Beethoven
was not at home, and the variations were left with a servant. The
further information that Beethoven played the work with his
nephew Karl, and approved of it, is indeed questionable: apart
from the fact that the composer's deafness would have proscribed
such an occupation, his approval could surely have been won
from a *reading* of Schubert's variations, as it was in later years by
a reading of Schubert's songs.

The French theme is not unpleasing in its rather old-fashioned,
plodding manner: it is an example of a type of song which Schubert himself largely destroyed. The shape of the melody is so
symmetrical, and its phrases are so balanced, as to suggest mere
contrivance.

Ex. 7

The rise and fall of bars 1–4 are repeated in bars 5–8, and the same
arching device is extended over the whole of the second half from
bars 9–16. The falling seconds of the penultimate bar are treated

individually by Schubert in his subsequent variations, the earliest instance of his singling out from a theme some feature for distinctive treatment. The feature, in any case, is his own, since these accented passing notes, falling step-wise to the tonic, are an embellishment of the original air. Schubert is responsible, too, for preserving the dotted rhythm of the opening 'anacrusis' throughout the theme, dispensing with the smooth quavers of his original. He accepts Drouet's harmonisation of the tune save that in one chord—in bar 14—the C sharp of the bass is changed to the more dramatic C natural.

The lay-out of the variations between the players is, as always in Schubert's pianoforte duets, beyond criticism. The large body of work which the composer left in this medium is notable; but it is not generally realised that he came comparatively late in his career to the medium, as, in fact, the medium itself came late in the history of music. Apart from the three fantasias of his boyhood, slight in worth but veritably enormous in bulk, the only work for pianoforte duet before these variations is the Rondo, Op. 138, which he composed in the January of this same year, supposedly for his friend Josef Gahy. The division of interest springs from the fact that 'Secondo' is usually given the theme, while 'Primo' adds the textural decoration which gives the variations their quality. And this quality is greatly superior to that of the preceding sets of variations, being more fluent, varied and riper than theirs. While these variations risk monotony by their close correspondence to what one might call the 'form' of the French air, and to the original common-time signature, they are saved by the wide choice of keys; the boldness of this key-scheme has already been described. But although the shape of the sixteen-bar theme still governs the course of most of the variations (with the anacrusis retained in every case), three of them, V, VII and VIII, reveal the unconventional break away from the pattern of the air, and in these three Schubert's fancy ranges with pleasant results.

Reference was made in chapter II to Schubert's use of delicate and unexpected chromatic harmony beneath a smooth, diatonic flow of melody. The same tenderness and warmth which such harmony gives to his songs are found also in these variations of Op. 10. Var. III, for example, introduces unexpected subdominant minor ninths below a simple C major version of the theme; their downward resolution is contrasted with the rising augmented seconds that occur later in the section. This is the variation which exploits the falling seconds in the 'Romance'; something of the mood and fashion of the piece come again in the attractive little 'Trauermarsch' belonging to the operatic fragment 'Adrast' which Schubert wrote a few months later.

His customary practice of accompanying a theme with a running bass movement, or superimposing on it flashing counterpoints, is to be found again; the former feature is vigorously used in var. II recalling by its steadfast, processional march the finale of the Octet in F major (Op. 166), and the 'Credo' section of the Mass in G major. The buoyancy and pianistic quality of the descant phrases give charm and distinction to this series. Throughout his work in the next few years, and especially in the masterpieces of 1824–1826, this charm and this distinction are native to his style, but they appear only spasmodically in the variations composed after 1826. In vars. I, IV and V the descant device is used, growing more intense until its full power is felt in var. VII.

As in the 'Ten Variations in F major' of 1815, Schubert seeks to give unity to the assembly of pieces by using in later variations figuration and motive derived from earlier ones. The triplet figure of the first variation is used freely for theme and accompaniment in var. V, and it becomes yet more important in var. VII, evolving there a marked 12/8 rhythm. Side by side with this growth is the treatment of a semiquaver scale passage from var. IV in var. VI and more pronouncedly in var. VII. This seventh variation, marked *più lento*, has, in fact, gathered to itself most of the typical ideas of the whole work, and their fusion required the breadth and scope that this penultimate variation is given. Its length, 37 bars, is a new departure for Schubert. There are still finer examples of this skilful fusion of ideas in the Fantasy for Pianoforte, Op. 15, of four years later, and in the Introduction to the variations on *Trockne Blumen*.

We have another example of the unifying device whereby the final variation is made a variant, so to say, of a previous one: the 'variation-pair' technique already discussed. The E major march of var. V appears once more in var. VIII, this time actually marked 'Tempo di marcia'. It is an ample and poetic version of its predecessor, and the mature Schubert storms into the closing bars, at the climax, with unforgettable effect. In this finale the triplet and semiquaver figures are not fused but contrasted; the music swells to a *ff* climax in E minor, and the billowing arpeggios of the bass remind us of the song *Rastlose Liebe*. Within the space of two bars the clanging harmony is hushed to a pianissimo and the melody is resumed in A flat major! Again the climax comes, again on the fortissimo E minor chord, but the quiet melody follows this time in the even remoter key of B flat major. From this key the cadence in E major is attained by proceeding through B flat minor and C sharp minor. The whole episode is as notable an adventure in tonality as any in Schubert.

The last variation comprises more than a third of the whole work, and carries on the departure from custom which was observed in var. VII. Its music lifts Op. 10 into the realm of

Schubert's minor masterpieces, and its vision influenced all that is out-standing in his subsequent work in variation form.

5. Introduction, Variations and Finale in B flat, Op. 82: no. 2 [D.603]

Pianoforte Duet. (?) 1818

No greater mystery surrounds any piece of Schubert's than that which shrouds these variations in B flat for pianoforte duet. Until 1860 their very existence was unknown. In that year Julius Schuberth & Co. (Hamburg and Leipzig) re-issued Schubert's Op. 82, the copyright of which they had acquired from Haslinger of Vienna. This opus is a set of variations in C major on a theme of Hérold's[1] and a work which had enjoyed a fair popularity. Schuberth & Co. called these C major variations Op. 82: no. 1 and included with them, as Op. 82: no. 2, a second set in B flat. No one has the remotest idea how the manuscript of this added set reached the firm of Schuberth's, nor where it had been during the forty or so years between its composition and its publication in Germany.

Kreissle's remarks in the supplement to his biography of the composer (English edition, vol. ii, p. 289) could be interpreted to mean that the Hamburg publishers had bought these B flat variations from Haslinger as well as the set in C major, but this cannot be so. Schubert's dealings with the Viennese firm date from as late as 1827. All his works published by Haslinger are late ones, the first being Op. 77, a set of dances called 'Valses Nobles' by the publisher; these were composed in late 1826 or early 1827. The set of variations which Schuberth & Co. called Op. 82: no. 2 is an early work of Schubert's, belonging possibly to 1818. It may have been written during the Zseliz period; it may even have been written during the following winter for Marie and Caroline Esterházy,

[1] See page 81.

since it is more than likely that Schubert continued, in Vienna, to give the two children pianoforte lessons.

Since nothing is known of the history of this piece, and since after its publication by Schuberth & Co. the manuscript disappeared, Nottebohm, in his Thematic Catalogue[1], listed it as a doubtful work. But it is unquestionably Schubert's. The style proclaims it to be an early work, and an inferior one at that, but passage after passage reveals his characteristic touch, and stamps it as authentic.

The Introduction exploits the tonality of B flat, and bold chords (*ff*) alternate with a jagged, rhythmic figure (*p*), until characteristically, the two elements combine into soft, lyrical phrases. Towards the close of the section there is a fascinating instance of the pervading influence of his great contemporary on his work of those years:

Ex. 8

Primo

Secondo

The original theme (*Moderato*, 2/4) is one of the shortest and simplest which he ever wrote for variations. It is sixteen bars long, with each half marked for repetition. It might be taken by any text-book as a flawless example of ternary form. That it belongs to the same period as the *Andante con moto* of the PF. Duet Sonata in B flat, Op. 30, of 1818 is very clear. There is a similar alternation of loud and soft chords in the middle section of the theme as was used in the introduction: this is one obvious way in which the work achieves a certain unity—there are other small details as well.

Four variations are based on the theme. As with the preceding work, Op. 10, the lay-out of the music between the players is admirable. The texture of his pianoforte duets has been compared by William Glock to a rich tapestry hanging from top to bottom of the keyboard, every strand of which has its own contribution to make to the effect of the fabric.

The first three variations merely fill out the contours of the theme, each one following closely the shape of the original as was Schubert's practice; each, as was also his practice, intensifies the ornamentation—the first with triplet, the second with quadruplet figures, and the third with a display of bravura and leaping octaves (it is marked *Brillante*). Var. III is the climax of the work. Schubert, having shown what can be done with flashing decoration, feeling perhaps that such decoration is part and parcel of variation form, now distils the poetry out of his theme. The extension of the melody in the fourth variation is excellent; the four-bar rhythm disappears, and the counterpoint above 'Secondo's' theme now expands into melodies of its own, now hints at the theme itself, now falls chromatically over the darker harmonies in the bass, and always with delicacy and grace.

A cadenza bar leads to the finale (*Vivace*, 3/8), which is not a variation on the theme but, like the Introduction, an independent movement. Like the Introduction, too, it shows a certain kinship with the variations in the contours of its theme. The theme bears a marked resemblance to that of the charming finale of his solo sonata in B major (August 1817):

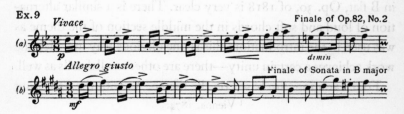

Ex. 9

but the two movements are not comparable in merit. In many ways, by jaunty *Ländler* rhythms, by chromatic progressions, by buoyant melodic periods, by the favourite shift to a key a major third below the tonic, the music tries to take wing; but the movement remains at only a moderate level, well written, adequate, and yet, in its total effect, perfunctory.

IV

THE SONG VARIATIONS: 1819–1824

6. Variations on *Die Forelle*, Op. 114.
7. *Adagio* from Fantasy in C major, Op. 15.
8. Introduction and variations on *Trockne Blumen*, Op. 160.
9. Variations from the Octet, Op. 166.
10. Variations on *Der Tod und das Mädchen*, Op. posth.

Schubert is the first composer of note who chose to write variations on his own songs,[1] and the only one to achieve worthy results by doing so. Perhaps the word 'chose' is dubious: the probability is that all five of his song variations were composed at the request of his associates. Four of the five sets occur in the period of which this chapter treats, and all are connected with friends, performers, or patrons: Sylvester Paumgartner, Emanuel von Liebenberg de Zsittin, Ferdinand Bogner and Josef Barth. (The remaining one of the five sets is found in the Fantasy, Op. 159, of 1827, and this is associated with the violinist Josef Slawjk. It is discussed in Chapter VI.) The fifth set of variations which belongs to the period under review is based on a duet from one of his operettas; the variations form a movement in the famous Octet, and this, also, has its patron, Ferdinand, Count Troyer, althought it can be stated with fair certainty that he could not have known of Schubert's operetta, and hence proposed the theme; indeed, a reason for its choice is hard to find.

---

[1] Haydn wrote variations for the so-called 'Emperor' Quartet, based on his setting of 'Gott erhalte Franz den Kaiser'; but even were the melody entirely his own, the setting is hardly a 'song' as the word is meant here.

During these years Schubert's songs were growing famous; it is a period in his life when Vogl chiefly, but many other lesser singers of the day, such as August von Gymnich and Franz Jäger, were introducing them to the Viennese public, in drawing-room and concert hall. Even so, one finds it difficult to see exactly why Schubert should have chosen, or allowed himself to be persuaded, to write variations on any of the particular songs for which he did so. Not one of them has a simple strophic form: from each of them he omitted material that adds some value to the specific song. In none of them, not even in *Die Forelle*, is the emotional content uncomplicated, or, better still, negligible. He makes no attempt whatever to match the moods of the variations with the mood of his song. Light hearted themes sponsor the same mixed variety of emotion as do the more solemn ones. Dr. Hans Gal has suggested that Schubert wrote these variations in order to develop the melodies more fully than he was able to do within the restricted framework of the songs. The idea would have more force if the results were all convincing; but apart from the variations on 'Death and the Maiden', and possibly those on 'Der Wanderer', the sets hardly support such a theory.

Except in the case of *Trockne Blumen* all the variations were composed some time after their respective songs, the 'Death and the Maiden' variations after an interval of seven years, and the Octet variations after an even longer period. The gaps in the sequence of variations—in 1820, in 1821 to late 1822, in 1823—are all due to his absorption in opera; even symphonies and chamber-works were also set aside in those years—but never, it is worthy of note, the songs. It is clear that Schubert was still reluctant to use variation-form for one of the four orthodox sonata-movements; only one of these sets is a quite independent piece, but two of the others form supplementary movements, and although a fourth set is actually the slow movement of a four-movement work, the work is called by Schubert a Fantasy.

If during his experimental years he clung unadventurously to the pianoforte for his variations, he certainly ranged farther afield during the 1819–1824 period; apart from the above-mentioned Fantasy (Op. 15) the song-variations are all for chamber-music combinations and we find in no other period such a variety of medium. In the later sets, in fact, only a single departure from the use of the pianoforte occurs, in Op. 159, and then merely for the combination of violin with pianoforte. All the sets of these years were published by 1875; it is hardly necessary to add that the opus numbers are completely meaningless as a guide to the order of composition.

6. Variations on the song *Die Forelle* from the Pianoforte Quintet in A major, Op. 114.   [D.667]

Pianoforte, violin, viola, cello and double-bass. Autumn 1819

Schubert's setting of the poem *Die Forelle* (*The Trout*) by Christian Schubart, composed in the spring of 1817, has been extremely popular from the first; this is vouched for in a number of ways: by the several copies in the composer's own hand which he wrote for his friends, by the numerous references to it in contemporary documents, by the many translations of its verses, and by its early publication and re-publication in Schubert's lifetime. The song first appeared as a supplement to the 'Wiener Zeitschrift' of 9 December 1820[1] and was published by Diabelli on 13 January 1825, eventually numbered Op. 32. Schubert's

---

[1] It was the third of Schubert's songs to be issued as a supplement before the actual publication of his work began in 1821. The other two songs were *Am Erlafsee* and *Widerschein*.

extant autographs of the song number five; the last was made in October 1821, and only then did he add the six-bar prelude to the song.

Not least among the tokens of its popularity is the fact that variations were composed on it. They appear as a supplementary movement in the Quintet in A major for pianoforte and strings, which may have been started at Steyr in 1819 during a summer visit to Upper Austria in the company of the singer, Johann Vogl, but was certainly completed in Vienna during the following autumn. Schubert's quintet is supposed, by a fairly reliable tradition, to have been commissioned by one Sylvester Paumgartner, an amateur cellist and a leading light in the music-making of the small town; it was, according to Albert Stadler's testimony, to be a companion to Hummel's Op. 87 for the same combination of instruments. Paumgartner is also said to have admired the song, *Die Forelle*, and to have requested variations on it. The Quintet was published posthumously by Josef Czerny of Vienna, in May 1829, as Op. 114.

In considering the development of the true pianoforte quintet in the nineteenth century, i.e. the combination of pianoforte with string quartet, Schubert is not, on the strength of this work, considered a forerunner. But if the attractive contrasting of tone-colour—pianoforte against a quartet of strings—is the chief *raison d'être* of the medium, then Schubert, equally with the later Romantics, deserves credit. More, in fact, than Schumann, who, in the whole of his Op. 44, wrote a mere half-a-dozen scattered bars in which the pianoforte is silent.

Thus, the theme of the song is announced by the quartet of strings alone. As is invariably the case when Schubert chose one of his songs as a basis for variations, the theme undergoes a transformation intended to render it more instrumental in form and flavour. In the case of *Die Forelle* the following modifications occur:

(*a*) The key of the song is D flat; this is changed to the—for strings—more congenial key of D natural.

(*b*) Several grace notes are added to the tune, and in general the smooth quaver and semiquaver rhythms are changed into dotted-note rhythms.

(*c*) The first half of the melody is marked for repetition.

(*d*) The tempo of the song is changed from *Etwas Lebhaft* (Rather Lively) to *Andantino*, and the slower pace counteracts the possibly jaunty effect of the additions in (*b*). A return is made to the former livelier tempo, now called *Allegretto*, in the finale of the variations.

It may be noted in connection with these changes that the more dramatic middle section of the song is omitted altogether from the 'Thema'.

There are five variations on the theme; the first three exemplify his usual methods with the form, that is, the theme is enriched and embellished with every conceivable ornamentation, scale figure and arpeggio. Never was music more utterly unselfconscious in its exuberant and reckless display. If these three variations are superior to anything that has preceded them in this style it is partly because of the perennial freshness and delight of the tune itself, and partly because Schubert, growing more confident in his technical ability in these matters, had never before handled such decorative passages so ably and attractively. This is noticeably so in the billowing use of broken chords in var. III. As always, the form of the tune *a a b* dominates the form of these variations.

But with the fourth variation there is the kind of departure which we have been led to expect from his work in Op. 10. There is a change into D minor and the growth of power in the preceding paragraphs reaches its climax in the fortissimo chords of the dramatic opening bars. Then comes a sudden and tense hush over the work; it is one of the earliest uses of a device which never failed in his later works to produce passages of the highest and most moving poetry. The singing phrases of violin and piano lead to a yet quieter music, and in the pianissimo codetta, wrought to perfection, cello, viola and violin sing their way to silence. Such a passage as this, with its close imitation between the instruments, charged with emotional and poetical qualities, is a feature of this quintet, and similar effects can be found in the contemporary Sonata in A major, Op. 120, e.g. bars 65–80 of the first movement. It is a development in Schubert's style which, appearing towards the close of his early period of growth, say 1818–1819, dominates the work of his maturity until in the last two years or so it undergoes yet a further development. Then, the contrapuntal episodes are not so much concerned with similar phrases in imitation as with the conjunction of different melodies.

It is in the closing bars of the fourth variation, if anywhere, that we get the slenderest hint of the middle section of the song.

The same tender mood inspires the opening of the last variation. The key hovers between B flat major and minor, and the tune passes through modulations which are extraordinarily steep:

The soft, songlike quality of the whole variation is undisturbed throughout; the phrases expand and flower into a most charming couplet of modulations: C sharp minor to a full close in A major, F sharp minor to a full close in D major.

The finale is simply an instrumented version of the song without any embellishment of the melody and with the quicker tempo restored. (Again the middle section is omitted.) The simplicity and brightness at the start of the finale after the soft darkness of the fifth variation create the same atmospheric effects as we find in the close of the song itself, and the intention is surely deliberate. It is enhanced by the appearance in the pianoforte part 'with charming, friendly effect'[1] of the amiable sextolets of the song, one of Schubert's most famous touches of accompaniment, suggesting, as it does, the swirl and leap of the trout. It is perhaps worth pointing out that this finale does not use the six-bar introduction, indicating that Schubert himself did not, at that period, admit its necessity.

The movement displays Schubert's growing development in the form, as the whole work displays his development in the wider fields of music itself. These variations showed him what could be done with his own songs, and prepared the way for the abiding excellencies of the variations he was to write in the next few years.

7. *Adagio* FROM THE FANTASY IN C MAJOR, OP. 15.   [D.760]

Pianoforte solo.   November 1822

It was stated in the previous section that when Schubert chose the melody of one of his songs as a basis for variations he modified it for his purpose. This is so in the work now to be discussed. The theme is selected from the setting of *Der Wanderer* which he composed in October 1816. The words of the famous song are by G. F. Schmidt of Lübeck, and first appeared during 1808 in a 'Pocket Book of Sociable Pleasures'.[2] Schubert is said (by Kreissle)

---

[1] Richard Capell, *op. cit.*, p. 136.

[2] Full particulars are given in Max Friedlaender's 'Supplement' to vol. i of Peters' edition of Schubert's Songs (p. 50–54).

to have had his attention drawn to the verses by a Viennese priest named Horni.

In the song at the verse commencing 'Die Sonne dünkt mich hier so kalt' appears the melody which Schubert used for variations in the *Adagio* movement of his Fantasy for pianoforte solo.

But this time the modifications are so marked that an almost new melody emerges. In fact, while engaged on the preliminary studies for this section, the present writer began to wonder whether the likeness between the two melodies was accidental.[1] Let the documentary evidence be considered before the musical facts are allowed to influence the verdict. Neither Schubert, nor his friends, his publishers, his reviewers, his critics, although all referred to the Fantasy in letters, memoirs, advertisements and books, ever named the 'Wanderer' in connection with it, or mentioned its treatment of the song. In view of the extraordinary popularity and fame of the song this is remarkable. Schubert's biographer, Kreissle (1865), never used the term, nor, significantly, did Liszt in his arrangement of the work for pianoforte and orchestra—he called it simply 'Grosse Fantasie'. The appellation 'Wanderer', linking the work to the song, first appeared quite late in the nineteenth century (*c.* 1873). Modern criticism, accepting the title without question, even goes so far as to suggest a programmatic interpretation of the work, seeing in Schubert's obvious melodic links between the *Adagio* and the other movements of the Fantasy, an underlying and morbid psychological significance, an aura of melancholy—'Die Sonne dünkt . . . so kalt, . . . die Blüthe welk, das Leben alt'. The view cannot be maintained against the evidence of the music itself—music as vivid and sanguine and inviting as Schubert ever wrote.

[1] See his article 'Schubert's "Wanderer" Fantasy' in the 'Musical Times', December, 1951.

The Fantasy was written for, as well as dedicated to Liebenberg de Zsittin, a wealthy landowner and a pupil of Hummel's, and this may account for its exalted pianistic style. It was published by Cappi & Diabelli on 24 February 1823 as Op. 15. Schubert was paid 50 florins for it (about £2) and the transaction was partly instrumental in causing the subsequent break between the composer and this firm. Two months after the publication of the work the 'Allgemeine Musikalische Zeitung' of Vienna said of the variation-movement:

'. . . the author comes forward with lovely melodies and besides offers the pianoforte player the opportunity of proving his agility in the most brilliant manner . . .'

The manuscript of the Fantasy, now in America, bears the date 'November 1822'. The work is thus contemporary with the 'Unfinished' Symphony and the same abundance of melody is found in the one as in the other. The *Adagio* movement is not, like nearly all other similar movements of his in variation-form, divided into numbered sections; each, as far as it is possible to distinguish it, flows without a break into the next. Even the theme is not separated from its derived variations. It consists of the eight bars in the song, simplified and given greater dignity, which are sung to the words:

Die Sonne dünkt mich hier so kalt,
Die Blüthe welk, das Leben alt,
Und was sie reden, leerer Schall,
Ich bin ein Fremdling überall.

(Here the sun seems so cold to me, the blossom withered, and life old, they all speak a meaningless language, for I am everywhere a stranger.)

The two melodies are quoted here for comparison:

Ex.11

Schubert's variation theme leads straightway into a homely and pleasant E major version whose close, four-part texture is strikingly like the *reprise* of the *Andante* in the String Quartet in A minor, Op. 29, (bars 69 *et seq.*). From hereon the music spreads into a broad-winged and spacious movement like nothing else in the composer's work until the very end when we find it again in the slow movement of the String Quintet. The pianistic writing is bold and elaborate, and almost overborne with ornament. The style was new in his keyboard writing and it was never entirely absent from subsequent works.

After the stormy tremolos of the second variation a C sharp major version of the melody sings out in great, sweeping octave phrases. Just as the E major variation seemed to be drowned by the surging tremolos of the second variation, so the song of the C sharp major episode is submerged by the fourth variation. This uses the harmony of the theme as a basis for a tumult of ornamental runs and scales and chords, the musical equivalent of the curlicues and arabesques of the baroque period in painting, which would be empty of interest save for one redeeming feature: this is the introduction of a figure which is to develop into the theme of the scherzo (Presto) which follows the variation movement:

Ex.12

The final pages show a remarkable amalgamation of elements from the preceding three variations: the tremolandos are heard softly, yet ominously, above the still billowing arpeggios of Ex. 12 (*a*); alternating with them are the sad, nostalgic phrases of the third variation. The conflict resolves and the movement ends with song-like cadences. Experiments of this kind in the variations of Op. 10 and of Op. 82: no. 2 have here produced a magnificent result.

It is difficult to dissociate entirely from this purely instrumental piece, using purely instrumental procedures, a naturalistic interpretation. Here is the Schubert of the Nature *Lieder* working on the scale of *Erlking* and *Waldesnacht* to produce, quite unintentionally, a picture of water and wind and storm and ensuing peace. He himself used almost identical keyboard figures in the accompaniment of the song *Iphigenia* (July, 1817) where they illustrate the words:

'Und die See, mit hohen Wellen, die an Klippen sich zerschellen, Uebertäubt mein leises Fleh'n.'

('And the ocean, with high waves, which dash themselves against the cliffs, deafens my soft prayer.')

The musical elements employed are very like those, for instance, of Wagner's in the Prelude to 'Die Walküre', and it is impossible in these days to rid the mind of such associations, however undesirable they may be.

It will be noted, in considering this *Adagio* in its entirety, how the procedure in the *Forelle* variations, the building up to a tremendous climax and the quieter fall of the closing variations, is used again. It becomes in all the subsequent sets of variations which contain work of value, with only one exception, a standard practice.

8. Introduction and Variations on the song *Trockne Blumen* from the song-cycle *Die schöne Müllerin*, Op. 160. [D.802]

Pianoforte and Flute.   January 1824

The refinement and sweetness of the song *Trockne Blumen* make it one of Schubert's secondary masterpieces; it has the fragile beauty of the flowers it celebrates, and the picture of the unhappy young miller, with his withered forget-me-nots, is outlined in the lightest of strokes. It is incredible that the composer should have used the melody as the basis of a set of showy and coruscating variations.

In Schwind's letter of 13 February 1824 to Schober we read:

'Schubert now keeps a fortnight's fast and confinement. He looks much better and is very bright, very comically hungry and writes quartets and German dances and variations without number.'

Since the manuscript of these variations for flute and pianoforte, now in the possession of the Vienna City Library, is dated 'January 1824', Schwind is undoubtedly referring to them in his letter. Schubert's 'bright' mood is present in the work. It was composed for the flautist Ferdinand Bogner whose connection with the Schubertian circle is due to his wife, Barbara Fröhlich. He was professor of the flute on the staff of the Musikvereinschule, in Vienna, and Schubert's offering is deliberately virtuoso in style. But why was it based on this particular song?

'. . . *Trockne Blumen* has a pathos that makes us grudge Schubert forgiveness for subsequently writing on it a set of variations,

E   S.V.

which was a bad thing to do; and writing them for the flute, which was worse; and making some of them brilliant, which was blasphemous.'

The words are Sir Donald Tovey's, and his censure is fully deserved. There was nothing, structurally, that could be done with the music of the song, so tenuous and self-sufficing. It is just possible that in the hands of a more calculating composer the moods of sadness and passionate longing might have been explored further, but Schubert, with complete insensibility to the emotional atmosphere he has himself evoked, falsifies both melody and meaning; the subsequent variations add nothing of significance, and for all their plunging movements into this mood or that, they never re-establish the truth.

Theme and variations are heralded by an introduction, and the music of these 37 bars is of true, if not first-rate, Schubertian quality. They open with a dragging, dactyllic rhythm, half pathetic, half despairing, another instance of the recurring influence of Beethoven's *Allegretto*. With an aptness later to be set aside by the variations the introduction dwells on the emotional climax of the song—the question to the tear-drenched flowerets: Ihr Blümlein alle, wovon so nass? But this phrase, as it stands in the song, is reached only after a slow re-shaping of the initial flute figure, and by devious keys, as if the lover were pondering the words of his question, expressing them in different ways and asking them with changed emphasis. The pathos is enhanced by the use of a new phrase which is woven into the texture of the music with careful art; the hope that never quite fades is embodied in a figure that derives from the end of the song—the valedictory address to the flowers of the coming spring. When the flute finally poses the lover's question, pianissimo, and in the key of the song, the pianoforte gathers up the materials of the previous bars,

Ex.13

and as the flute utters its question again and again, the moods of hope, despair and heart-ache pass rapidly through the music of the pianoforte and so lead to the theme itself.

We have noticed in earlier sets of variations Schubert's growing skill in this kind of fusion of ideas, and it is unfortunate that the method was not used, and to an equally fine effect, in the variations which have been so introduced, but the integrity of the music of the introduction as a commentary on the song we know in the song-cycle is one matter; what actually follows, as the theme is announced, is another.

The wrong psychological note is struck at the outset:

Ex.14

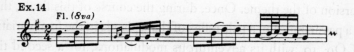

The placing of the slurs, the staccato touch on the end quavers, the flippant grace-notes: could vandalism go further? The answer, unhappily, is yes, for Schubert proceeds to heap more indignities on his song-theme. The questioning phrase, so touchingly developed in the Introduction, becomes:

Ex.15

and although the E major ending of the song follows unchanged, these falsifications rob it of all the elfin quality so memorable in the song.

But if bad begins, worse remains behind. The variations certainly exhibit a growth, not of character or feeling, but of virtuoso technical resource. Schubert flings in all he knows, and it is in this welter of poverty-stricken key-board figuration that he reveals what has been called his 'half-mastery of the instrument', rather than in the demands which he makes on the player of his sonatas and impromptus.

One turns the blackening pages in despair, knowing that beneath these rioting scales and jaunty rhythms, the essential Schubert is lost; one will find no magic here—only conjuring tricks. With each succeeding variation, there are seven in all, the theme becomes more debased. The penultimate one is a hopping 3/8 movement in C sharp minor, similar in style to the final variations of the set in F major and of the set on the Hüttenbrenner theme, and it leads without a break into the last variation. This is a quick-march in E major based on yet another, fortunately the last, perversion of the theme. Once, during the course of this finale, there is a passing gleam, a pale reflex of that episode in the final variation of Op. 10, with its adventurous modulations; for a second time the music sinks, after a climax, to a hushed *piano*. Instead of the expected resolution, the tonality takes a completely unforeseen turn, and the low flute phrases have some dignity. But these are brushed aside for the final peroration.

It is significant that this work, almost entirely devoid of worth, deliberately departs from the method of working up to a climax, and then subsiding to a quiet and poetical close; a method which Schubert so notably used in the variations of Op. 15, and is to use regularly in those sets of variations which bear the impress of his genius.

That he wrote this work on the eve of composing the variations in the String Quartet in D minor and those of Op. 35, is almost unbelievable. The feeling is inescapable that for once in his life his unwavering loyalty to the integrity of his own genius was set aside, and for the sake of effect, and perhaps to ingratiate his work with the famous flautist, he was ready to pile empty virtuosity on one of his most delicate and sincere songs: and then to do it badly!

9. VARIATIONS FROM THE OCTET, OP. 166.   [D.803]

Two violins, viola, cello, double-bass, clarinet, horn and bassoon.   February 1824

The theme of these variations comes from the twelfth number in the composer's operetta *Die Freunde von Salamanka* (libretto by Johann Mayrhofer), which was written eight years previously, from 18 November to 31 December, 1815. It is a duet for two subsidiary characters, Laura and Diego ('Gelagert unter'm hellen Dach der Bäume...').

The variations constitute the fourth movement of the celebrated Octet which was commissioned by Ferdinand, Count Troyer, an official in the establishment of the Archduke Rudolph. Troyer was a noted clarinettist and it is clear that the commissioned work gives much scope to his instrument, without allowing it to emerge too prominently. The Octet was finished on 1 March 1824, and performed soon afterwards at Troyer's residence in Vienna, a house owned by Baron von Spielmann.

It was published in an incomplete form by the firm of Spina, in March 1853: the variation-movement and the minuet were omitted (a mutilation which caused it to fit the Procrustean bed of ortho-dox four-movement structure). The full work appeared some twenty years later than that. The manuscript is now in the Vienna City Library.

It is well known that Schubert's work is modelled on the Septet (Op. 20) of Beethoven, possibly because of a hint on the part of its 'onlie begetter'; the connections between the two works are many and interesting, and while the obvious ones—correspondence between movement and movement, similar bar-lengths and so on—are familiar and have been tabulated, there are also several more obscure links which have been quite unexplored.

We think of the Septet as one of Beethoven's early works and of the Octet as one of the products of Schubert's maturity: it is overlooked that when Schubert wrote the Octet he was several years younger than Beethoven at the time of the composition of the Septet.

Although there can be no answer one cannot avoid asking the question—'Why did Schubert resort to this rather ordinary theme from one of his more obscure operettas, written so many years previously?' If there be any possible answer it may be found in his chosen model; Beethoven's variation theme is supposed to derive from a Rhenish folk-song, and Schubert's theme has the same folk-song like quality. Otherwise there is not much else to commend it.

Something of the triviality, show and contrivance of the previous set of variations linger in this movement. But the greater depths hinted at here and there point to what is to come.

There is only a partial return to the principle of the central climax followed by a slackening of the tension until the quiet coda is reached. But the stress and conflict are not shown by increasing gradations of sound—it is remarkable how muted is the progress of these variations—but by a growing complexity of texture and instrumentation. The only f's in the work occur in vars. V and VI, and are of short duration; most of the movement is marked *p* and *pp*, but only in the coda do we find the scoring and ornate accompaniments thinning, and the air, as it were, clearing.

The theme, announced by strings and clarinet, is 32 bars long (with repeats) and represents a shortened version of the first part of the duet in the operetta. The key (C major) and time-signature (2/4) remain as in the duet, but the tempo *Andantino* was changed to *Andante* for the theme of the variations.

There are seven of these, and they consist of mere ornamentations of the theme, but there are welcome departures from the text at the end of vars. VI and VII. At first the tonic key of the opening persists, vars. I–IV all being written in C major. The rather mechanical means by which each variation is made slightly more complex than the one which precedes it contributes little that appeals; the congeniality of the theme must bear the whole burden of holding the listener's interest. The same devices were more successful in the variations on *Die Forelle* since in that movement they were applied to a more attractive and likeable theme—more attractive to the composer, it is felt, as well as to the listener.

Even the introduction of the minor key (C minor) in var. V brings no charm or imagination into the work. It has been mentioned already that it seems as if Schubert felt in duty bound to enrich and embroider his theme in the first few variations before allowing his fancy to free itself from the fetters of a conventional procedure. The freeing comes at length with var. VI; a flowing, A flat version of the theme on the viola is made to serve as an accompaniment, and above this the clarinet and violin initiate passages of imitation which are taken up by the cello and bassoon, and finally a sextet of instruments begins to weave a pattern of vital and melodious counterpoint which might well be cited as evidence of Schubert's powers as a contrapuntist. The music grows even more charming and delicate until the end of the pattern is reached. But Schubert cannot stop: the impetus of his imaginative flight carries on beyond the orthodox double bar-lines for another fourteen bars while the attractive interplay of his derived motives produces the best music of the movement:

Ex.16

Had the movement ended here we should have been spared the discomfort of the concluding variation. This reverts to the tonic key and is marked *un poco più mosso*. An extremely trite version of the theme is accompanied by vulgar repeated chords on bassoon and horn while the violins add a giddy *bravura* of demisemiquaver runs. The distasteful episode over the music returns to *più lento* and achieves a coda of some dignity and even pathos. In the closing bars the horn sounds a throbbing pedal-note and is in unison with the double bass: perhaps the only instrumental touch of interest in the movement. But the sound of those *più mosso* bars, lingering in the ear, almost neutralizes the effect of poetry and beauty in the close.

10. VARIATIONS ON THE SONG *Der Tod und das Mädchen* FROM
    THE STRING QUARTET IN D MINOR, OP. POSTH.   [D.810]

    2 violins, viola and cello.   March, 1824

Schubert's song, *Der Tod und das Mädchen*, was composed in February, 1817 and published by Cappi & Diabelli on 27 November 1821 as part of the composer's Op. 7. Although without documentary evidence, such as that associated with *Die Forelle*, to prove the fact, its popularity was immediate: there is

Spaun's entirely imitative poem *Der Jüngling und der Tod*, set by Schubert soon afterwards, to vouch for this, and there is the evidence afforded by the autograph of the song, which, in later years, was cut up by Schubert's half-brother, Andreas, and sold piecemeal to collectors.

The variations were composed seven years after the song, not as a subsidiary movement for the second string quartet of his maturity, but as the important slow movement of the work. Eminently fitting to the grandeur and spaciousness of the whole work, they yet serve as an admirable foil to the vigour and impetuosity of the other movements. This much granted, it is groundless to urge further that the whole quartet is designed round the 'subject' of the song-text—the inexorable but consolatory figure of Death, and that the emotional aura of the variations likewise surrounds the other three movements. To argue thus means to turn a deaf ear to half-a-dozen incongruities in those three movements: the happy, lilting second subject of the *Allegro*, the rhythmic humour of the Scherzo, the placid contentment of the Trio-section, the grace and poetry of the finale. A chance resemblance in the last movement to a mere fragment of the melody of the *Erlking* has been made much of, far too much. That each of the four movements is in a minor key has also been adduced as evidence for the 'Death' impulse of the quartet. This last point might be examined a little more closely. It is quite common to find Schubert choosing for the Scherzo, as well as for the finale, of a work, the key of his first movement—a score of examples could be given; the scheme occurs in the string quartet under discussion. Since for this work the first movement is in a minor key, and since his slow movement is perforce in a minor key also, the result is inevitable, but not, therefore, deliberated.

For many years the String Quartet in D minor was relegated to

1826, but the discovery of part of the autograph, the first movement and most of the second, revealed the date to be March, 1824. The first performance took place on 1 February 1826 in Vienna, at the residence of Josef Barth, a singer and a friend of Schubert's, to whom the composer had dedicated the part-songs of Op. 11. For the performance Schubert revised the quartet (but clearly only superficially) and that is why the date 1826 was given to the work, and is still associated with it. It was published posthumously by Czerny of Vienna in July, 1831.

The theme of the variations is a pastiche of elements taken, or derived from the song: the 'Maiden's' melody is ignored altogether. The modifications and alterations are accordingly the most fundamental which the composer made in any of his song-themes, even more so than in that of *Der Wanderer*, yet the kinship between the theme of the variations and the song itself is close and obvious. The form of the theme is *a b c*; *a* is the pianoforte prelude of the song, *b* is newly-composed and does not appear in the song at all, *c* is the end of the melody sung by 'Death'. As with the majority of the songs of those years, an essentially diatonic theme is given depth by chromatic harmony, sometimes quite unexpected, yet now indissociable from the melody. Especially poignant is the diminished seventh towards the end of the phrase *b*, with the E natural in the bass, and the dominant seventh of D major later on; these chords are to provide the climaxes and excitements of nearly all the following sections. The key of the song is D minor: this was changed to G minor for the instrumental variations. The tempo too is, or should be, different from that of the song; the *Andante con moto*, 2/2, of the quartet, is slightly quicker than the song's *Mässig* (*Moderato*), 4/4.

The five variations are not numbered, but unlike those in the Fantasia, Op. 15, they are self-contained and are all marked for repeat. If all these repeat-signs are observed the movement is too long, and would take, in fact, about twelve minutes to play. With repeats the theme is 48 bars long, and its *basic* structure, as was the case in the Octet movement, is rigidly observed in every variation; but, unlike the variations in the Octet, there is no slightest deviation. The keys also are singularly non-adventurous: four variations are in G minor, one in G major. All this, on the face of it, is a reversion to his earliest manner, to an even stricter denial than in the earliest works, but the obstacles are triumphantly surmounted and although Schubert has dispensed with these external aids to stimulus and invention he has produced within his inflexible framework a music of such power and variety that the movement has won an admiration and an affection unequalled by any other of his compositions in this *genre*.

A return is made in the movement to the structure of a powerful climax (reached in var. V and almost immediately quitted, *cf.* the exactly similar procedure in the variations on *Die Forelle*), and a 'dying fall' in the coda—a scheme so lamentably lacking in the *Trockne Blumen* set. The music exemplifying the decline and relaxation is very characteristic: the minor key returns, the semiquavers give way to triplets, and these in turn to throbbing quavers; the quavers, by syncopated rhythms, merge into crotchets, and the coda ends with the *alla breve* movement of the opening. The method was used again, and was to be equally successful, in the first movement of the Sonata in A minor, Op. 42, of the following year.

The influence of the several sets of variations for pianoforte-duet seems to be felt in the lay-out of these variations for the medium of the string quartet. Apart from the announcement of the text, and the brief coda, the first violin, surprisingly, never plays the melody. Instead it adorns, and does so with the most delicious filigree decoration of any of the descant passages in his variations. It is interesting to see the difference in style between the treble counterpoints for pianoforte and these for violin. The runs and scale figures of the former are replaced by broken chords and octaves lying across the strings, more suitable to violin technique, and certainly more congenial to the player. The decorative setting provided for each variation is of superb quality, the finest example he gave of a vital and integrated use of conventional ornaments. This is made possible perhaps by the nature of his subject, which is, after all, largely a harmonic scheme.

His use of the medium for colour effects is at its best in the first movement of the quartet, but in these variations the cello contributes several examples of 'horn' timbre; in var. II the viola takes over the bass of the harmonies while the cello utters the theme (or something like it: a characteristic of these variations) sounding as a horn might amongst the other three instruments. It is treated with great freedom, and with magnificent effect, in var. V:

Ex. 17

A feature of Schubert's quartet-writing—the 'conversational' duet between violin and cello gives rise to points of interest in the third variation. The imitations between the outside parts in these 48 bars are of three entirely different types, a short, song-like passage, loud alternating chords spread across the strings, and a soft, fanfare figure derived from the main idea of the variation. This diversity is possible because of the incessant and unvarying rhythm of the inner parts. The whole of the middle variation is of the highest merit; it will be seen how the hammering rhythms at the start, marked *ff*, yield to a quiet and lyrical derivative, in the same fashioning as was first tried in the Introduction to the variations in B flat, Op. 82: no. 2.

The fourth variation is like a meditation on the text in G major; again it is difficult to trace the connection between the flow of the melody here and the main theme. This set of variations, indeed, might be compared to many of the composer's songs in the 'modified strophic' style, where the tunes of each stanza, although clearly akin, are yet subtly differentiated. The grace-notes which embroider the parts in var. IV are a vital part of the counterpoints, and much in advance of the use of them in the *Forelle* variations. It should be observed how Schubert distinguishes between the fall of the accent in ♪ as opposed to the fall in ♩♪ (a matter of importance, also, in the sonata movement already mentioned).

This *Andante con moto* is full of that 'Innigkeit' which is so typical of the composer's masterwork, and of the near-pathos that inevitably accompanies it. The movement is the first triumphant result of all his experiments, successful or otherwise, in the preceding sets of variations. Every one of them contributes some factor to the success of these 'Death and the Maiden' variations, and they, in turn, are to lead eventually to Op. 35.

V

MATURITY: 1824–1826

11. Variations on an original theme in A flat, Op. 35.
12. *Andante poco moto* from Sonata in A minor, Op. 42.
13. *Andantino varié*, Op. 84: no. 1.

The period covered by this chapter was, in general, the happiest in Schubert's life. His health, although undermined, benefitted considerably by the long summer holidays spent at Zseliz and Steyr; his work was becoming more widely known and freely published; his finances allowed him the freedom for which he craved; an enthusiastic circle of friends gave him the personal encouragement and admiration which was, for him as for all creative artists, a necessity.

The maturity and greatness of the variations of this period are due to the fact that he was now the master of the form and no longer mastered by it. In a sense these three sets are experimental works, but there is achievement as well as aspiration in them. The incredible thing is that there should have been no fulfilment of the promises held forth in these masterpieces.

They are all based on original themes; that is to say, on themes specially written for their variations, since it is now fairly well established that the so-called 'French motif' of Op. 84: no. 1 is actually Schubert's own composition.

The three sets were written for pianoforte, and in the second one, the slow movement of Op. 42, we have the first example of his use of a theme in his favourite triple time—and almost the last: there is only one more example, the variations of 1827 on *Sei mir gegrüsst*.

All three works were published in his lifetime, each one very shortly after its composition, and all within eighteen months or so of one another.

11. Eight Variations on an original theme in A flat, Op. 35. [D.813]
Pianoforte Duet. July 1824

'We believe that happiness exists for us in the place where once we were happy, but it really exists only in ourselves, and although I was sorely disillusioned, and renewed here an experience already undergone at Steyr, yet I am now more in a position to find happiness and peace in myself than I was then. A grand Sonata, and Variations on an original theme, both for 4 hands, which I have already composed, will serve you as a proof of this. The Variations have enjoyed a quite notable success.'

So Schubert wrote to his brother, Ferdinand, during July, 1824, from Zseliz. The eight variations, on an original theme, were clearly popular and successful in the Esterházy household, for later on, in August, he wrote to his friend Schwind in similar terms: 'I have composed a grand Sonata, and Variations, for 4 hands, which latter are enjoying a notable success here.' Early in 1825, in Vienna, Schwind heard the work for himself, and wrote of it to Schober in an enthusiastic fashion: 'The new variations for 4 hands are something quite extraordinary. The theme is as grandiose as it is languid, as purely set—don't laugh—as it is free and noble. In eight variations these pages are quite independently and vitally developed, and yet each again seems to reveal the theme.'

The work was published as Op. 35 by Sauer & Leidesdorf, in Vienna, on 9 February 1825, and dedicated by Schubert to

Count Anton Berchtold.[1] As with all of Schubert's works published by this firm, the manuscript was subsequently lost.

It has already been mentioned that there is a kind of parallelism between the works composed at Zseliz in 1818 and those composed in 1824. This set of variations corresponds to those of Op. 10 in kind: the medium, the number of variations, the style, to which we could apply Schwind's term 'grandiose' save that the word has now only a derogatory sound, and the technical means employed, all demonstrate the fact; even the themes of the two sets have something in common, the identical rhythmic anacrusis for instance. But not in degree: those six vital years in Schubert's development had deepened the content, amplified the resource, and wholly individualised the melody, the poetry and the poignancy of his music. There is no greater masterpiece amongst Schubert's compositions for pianoforte duet than Op. 35; not even the 'Grand Duo', its far more celebrated contemporary, surpasses it.

The theme, *Allegretto*, has no need of its label 'original' for it speaks its composer in every note: it is in Schubert's *alla Marcia* vein, hence, in all probability, Schwind's term 'grandiose', but his qualifying 'languid'[2] is a little difficult to understand. There is richness, there is the unmistakable Schubertian wistfulness and appeal, but the theme has nothing at all apathetic about it. It is more elaborately conceived than is usual with his variation themes; his fertile and spontaneous imagination seems unable to wait, but pours out its abundance from the start. Even a touch of canonic imitation is used in the second part of the melody. The form is

---

[1] O. E. Deutsch states that the two men were not in close touch, and hence the dedication was probably paid for. ('Schubert Documents', p. 399 f.)

[2] Schwind's word is *schmachtend*, which, in this context, could mean 'heart-felt' or 'highly emotional'.

a b a c, the last section forming a kind of *Abgesang* or codetta; the canon in *b* re-appears in, and influences, nearly all the subsequent variations. The Beethoven dactyllic rhythm is present: in the theme it has a dotted quaver modification, but even this disappears later.

The first four variations, as with those in the D minor String Quartet and elsewhere, follow the familiar pattern; none shows any divergence from the key, time-signature or structure of the theme. The decorative work grows more intense as we proceed, and his usual technical means of elaboration are to be found. But the elevated thought, the unfailing ingenuity of musical development, whereby every strand in the texture is alive and calls for the highest achievement on the part of the players, and the sensitive interplay of emotional stress and relaxation, these are new in his variations, a contribution from the instrumental masterpieces of that wonderful year. So, too, the counterpoint, which informs every bar of the work, is almost unexampled in his pianoforte music, and is admirably bent to the purpose of enrichment.

And did ever composer before him enrich as Schubert enriches here? The music is crammed with excellencies—almost too much so, for certainly the listener alone cannot be aware of all that is passing. Bach is the composer whom this music recalls again and again,[1] by the precision, by the sustained pattern-work, by the architectural sweep of the music, by the contrapuntal thought; in var. IV, particularly, he is almost physically present:

Ex. 18

Primo

<hr>

[1] It is important to note that Schubert was playing the 'Wohltemperirtes Klavier' Fugues that summer, possibly as part of his work with the Esterházy daughters. We know this from his brother Ferdinand's letter of 3 July 1824: '. . . I have today handed in the Bach fugues . . . for transmission to you.' (See O. E. Deutsch's 'Schubert Documents', pp. 359, 361.)

But nowhere is this ornament devoid of emotion. The derived melody in var. III, so tender and Schubertian, may be worked in free canon, but it could easily come from one of his most intimate and heartfelt songs. And var. V is simply a pure *Lied*. Here the key changes to A flat minor, and above soft arpeggios the lovely melody hovers. The Beethoven rhythm over-rides the dotted quaver effect; his influence is starkly obvious:

Ex. 19

A characteristic leaning to the Neapolitan key-relationship of A major gives beauty and pathos to the closing bars of the section.

The *maestoso* var. VI combines elements from early variations in a manner which recalls Op. 10 and Op. 15; the latter work is strongly suggested, but surpassed in interest.

The peak of the work comes in the next variation, and here, for the first time, there is a break with the dominating twenty-four bar organisation of the theme. This seventh variation, *più lento*, is one of the sublimest paragraphs in Schubert, in all music: it is infinitely tender in mood and simple in texture, and the chromatic harmony and modulation are, for their period, interesting in the extreme. The emotional tension rises, and then subsides in a sustained passage in G major (the main key is F minor); again Bach is recalled, this time it is the close of the 'Crucifixus' in the Mass in B minor, and this quintessential episode of Schubert's is worthy to stand comparison with that supreme passage. One of the composer's extraordinary cadences closes the variation; one feels in the treatment of this cadence that Schubert was searching after a new way with old harmonies. It was a way that future composers never explored: the methods of Wagner, for instance, were a break away into new paths.

The last variation, the eighth, is long (again we are reminded of
Op. 10) and forms the finale of the work. The unintermitting peroration is similar to those of earlier sets. But in this one the flame
of his inspired fancy is at its brightest, and although, externally,
this finale resembles half-a-dozen others and the means have been
used so often before, the content glows with a fiery enthusiasm
and power. We might have been given again the somewhat perfunctory and jaunty movement of a *Ländler* (hardly disguised by
the 12/8 of the time-signature), but as the two preceding variations
show, Schubert was writing at the top of his bent, and he cannot,
as the saying goes, put a foot wrong. Nowhere does he surpass
the spontaneous and joyful outpouring of this variation; it is a
picture of June in that Hungarian valley, sweet and sappy, full of
light and colour, of moving airs and changing skies. The melodies
rise and sparkle on the urgent rush of the music like sunlight on
water.

Ex. 20

and again:

Ex. 21

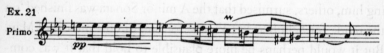

From A flat the music turns into A major, and with a new
impetus as if the flood of song will never cease. The tonal shifts
are like changing lights on a landscape—the constant form dis-
solves and seems to alter as we look. The end comes with *ff* tonic
and dominant chords, the only example among his mature sets of
variations in which the quiet close is dispensed with, and the
movement brought to a conclusion with confidence and vigour;
we stop, as it were, on the threshold of high summer.

12. *Andante poco moto* FROM THE SONATA IN A MINOR, OP. 42.
[D.845]

Pianoforte Solo.   Early 1825

The exact date of this composition is unknown since the auto-graph manuscript is lost. It was certainly composed in the early months of 1825 as we can see from a famous reference to it by the composer himself in a letter to his father and step-mother written on 25/28 July, 1825. He was on holiday in Steyr at the time with his friend, the singer Vogl, and he wrote: 'Especial pleasure was given by the variations from my new Pianoforte Sonata, which I myself played, and not without success, for several people assured me that the keys sang under my hands, and this, if it be so, pleases me greatly, because I cannot abide that cursed hacking, which is found even with distinguished pianoforte players, for it pleases neither the ear nor the heart.'

The Sonata in A minor, Op. 42, is usually considered (without any documentary evidence) to have been written *after* the un-finished sonata in C, the so-called 'Reliquie', which does survive in MS. and is dated 'April 1825'. Accordingly Grove, and, follow-ing him, others, surmised that the A minor Sonata was finished 'on the road', for Schubert left Vienna for Steyr in the middle of May. But it would perhaps be more plausible to hold that it was com-posed and completed before the 'Reliquie' was started and that the latter remained unfinished simply because Schubert did leave Vienna. In that case he would have taken with him the earlier, completed work, and this belongs, by such reasoning, to March or early April. The fact that Schubert in the letter quoted above calls it 'new' cannot necessarily mean that it had only just been finished: even a sonata by Schubert could remain, surely, in his view, 'new' for a few months!

The work was published early in 1826 by Pennauer of Vienna, as 'Première Grande Sonate'. It was 'première' only in the sense that it was the first sonata of Schubert's to be published. He dedicated it to Cardinal Rudolph, Archduke of Austria. Two periodicals, the Leipzig 'Allgemeine Musikzeitung' (1 March 1826) and the Frankfurt 'Allgemeine Musikanzeiger' (26 August 1826), reviewed the work with sympathy and admiration. Of the variation-movement, which is our chief concern, the first said:

'Second Movement: *Andante poco moto*, C major, 3/8—A simple, songful, gently serene theme, freely imagined and harmonised, with pleasant fluency in all four parts. It is all the more agreeable at this particular juncture, when it makes its effect most suitably. It is varied five times in the course of the movement, freely but not discursively in the matter of expression, and the final variation is worked into a developed coda. The harmony too is pure and clear. The whole resembles in its invention, expression and workmanship the *andantes* with variations in the quartets of Haydn's later years; and everyone knows that that implies no small praise.'

The theme, all that the Leipzig paper says of it, and of the utmost delicacy, is, with repeats, 48 bars long, and constitutes a miniature rondo. It passes freely from alto to treble and back again, and the texture hovers between three- and four-part harmony and bursts of full chords, in true pianistic fashion. We are reminded of his songs, of *An die Nachtigall* or *Du bist die Ruh'*. The five variations which follow are not numbered, and the above review goes a little astray when it says that the final variation is 'worked into a developed coda'. The coda, eighteen bars long, derives from the final variation, but is independent of it.

The variation-theme contains a plentiful use of appogiaturas, accented passing-notes and suspensions: the aim of the composer is to avoid over-suavity. As with other sets of his variations, this prominent feature of the theme colours and characterizes the succeeding variations; it is especially noticeable in var. III, where the clash of minor seconds and discordant progressions, brought about by the introduction of the Neapolitan sixth, drives the music to its climax. In like manner the sudden drop, in bar 24 of the theme, to the simplicity of the opening, after a momentary excitement, is used several times in the movement, each time with the same telling effect.

This set of variations is altogether more modest than the preceding one, that of Op. 35; it forms one movement of a sonata and consequently does not aim at the length or scope of the former work. But for all that this sonata movement represents the peak of the composer's achievement in the form of variations. Examination of the movement reveals a ripe fulfilment of previous experiments and promises new developments. These developments, it is true, were not carried further in the final variation essays which he was yet to write. The best of these, the *Andantino varié* of Op. 84, and the Impromptu in B flat, are not entire reversions to his early variation-style; they show unmistakably the effect of this set in Op. 42. But Schubert did not write in them, nor did he live long enough to give us, after them, the work which might have crowned his new departures in this remarkable set.

To begin with, there is a relinquishing of the unvarying practice of the previous few years whereby each of the earlier variations is made rather more elaborate than the preceding one; in fact, the second variation is as ornate as any of the rest. Both in this variation, and in var. IV, the florid adornment is saved from *bravura* by reason of its being made an integral part of the texture. The subsidiary phrases in the figuration are developed, passed from hand to hand, and emerge or recede according to musical demands and not to those of display.

There is, too, a considerable independence in each section. No linking ideas bind one to the other as we have seen happening before; unity is achieved in a quite new fashion, by anticipating in the closing bars of a variation the mood and style of the next one. Each seems thereby the inevitable outcome of what has gone before.

Even more important: we shall find that the usual adherence to the cadential pattern of the theme is whittled down to mere observance of its phrase-lengths, and there is an entirely novel treatment in the last three variations, in that each is based, not on the contours and harmonic unfolding of the theme, but upon a new subject derived from that theme or from part of it. This is the real, modern variation style appearing for the first time in his work. To take the finest of the five episodes as an instance: the 'subject' of var. III is here quoted against the opening bars of the theme of the variations:

Ex. 22

Theme only

(a)

Var. III

(b)

The course of this variation is then determined by its own subject and bears no relationship to the course of the theme of the variations.

As for var. IV, it is difficult to see more than the slenderest connection with the theme—it is based, apparently, on a fragmentary phrase from the middle bars—and this is an incredible, a unique thing to find in Schubert's variations. It is an indication of the distance he has travelled from—to take one instance—the 'Trout' variations. This fourth variation, in A flat, using vigorous scale passages with the hands an octave apart, scales which explode into powerful chordal progressions, is closely related to the slow movement of the contemporary sonata, the 'Reliquie'. There are also hints of rhythmic syncopations which are to be used more fully during the following year in the *Andante* of the Sonata in G major, Op. 78.

In the fifth and last variation we again look forward to the slow movement of Op. 78: this time in the sudden elaboration of a note or two in the melody (*cf.* bars 25 and 26 from the end of the variation, and bar 3 in Ex. 22 above). The variation provides another example of organic growth from an initial, derived subject, a growth which remains largely uninfluenced by the theme.

A word may be added on the coda, which brings the work to a subdued close, an example of the 'expiring flame' to use Sir Donald Tovey's words from his description of Schubert's codas in general. It forms an important phase in a feautre of the composer's style which has, strange to say, received no notice: namely, the addiction in his instrumental works of the last years of his life, to the plagal cadence. The hint of subdominant harmony in this coda leads to the effective use of this touching cadence in the last bar. The initial uses of the plagal cadence, of which this is one, were to lead eventually to the sublime Trio-section of the String Quintet in C major, written towards the end of his life.

13. *Andantino varié*, ON FRENCH MOTIVES, OP. 84: NO. 1. [D.823]
     Pianoforte Duet.   Early 1826
     This work was intended by Schubert to form the middle movement of a 'Divertissement in E minor' for pianoforte duet, of which the first and last movements are a *Tempo di marcia* and an *Allegretto*. The Viennese firm of Thaddäus Weigl, however, pub-

lished his first movement on 17 June 1826 as Op. 63, and by the
time the rest of the 'Divertissement' appeared, on 6 July 1827, the
original plan was either dropped, or lost sight of; the second and
third movements appeared together as Op. 84: nos. 1 and 2. The
irresponsible action of the publisher led to the severance of the
first movement from the others for nearly fifty years; the connection between the two opus numbers was not even noticed, although the fact that the 'March' had been called 'Op. 63: no. 1'
might have led to enquiries as to what had become of the rest of
the opus. The truth was re-established by Mandyczewski in the
'Revisionsbericht' to the 'Gesamtausgabe' of the composer's
works (Serie IX: nos. 21 and 22).[1]

All three movements were published with the information that
they were composed on 'original French motives'; these have never
been identified and it seems reasonable to suppose that they are of
Schubert's own invention. His idea may have been to give the
pieces an increased market value, or possibly to gloss the prevailing minor-key scheme. The variation-movement was called by
him *Andantino*, and the qualification *varié* was almost certainly the
publisher's.

The work belongs to a period in which Schubert wrote many
pianoforte duets, none of much importance; this *Andantino* is the
best of them. It was also a period of some remarkably fine songs,
among them the settings of poems from Goethe's novel 'Wilhelm
Meister' which comprise Schubert's Op. 62. The introspection
and despondency of these songs, and their consolation, are found
also in this variation-movement. In one case the connection is
very close: the melodic structure, the harmony, even the key, B
minor, of the *Andantino* theme are very like those in the duet for
soprano and tenor 'Nur wer die Sehnsucht kennt', Op. 62: no. 1,

[1] From a hint in Nottebohm's Thematic Catalogue.

called 'Mignon and the Harper'. There is a wistful quality, a resignation in the pianoforte and vocal duets, which is one characteristic of Schubert's style in 1825–26: it is very marked in the slow movement of the String Quartet of June 1826. The quality deepens in the 'Winterreise' to tragedy, and this is not without its effect on the major work of his last year, but then it is allied to an unearthly tranquillity. In so far as it is possible to identify the emotions with the musical means by which they are achieved, we may note the recurrence of a phrase which moves in steps from the minor third down to the leading note; it is here exemplified in the *Andantino* theme:

Ex. 23

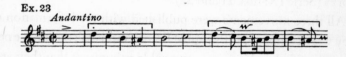

The theme has the simplicity of the mature artist; a simplicity quite unlike that of Op. 82: no. 2 for example, which belongs to Schubert's early years. There is the same distinction in the song *Wiedersehn* of 1825, which externally resembles many of the simple nature songs of 1815–1816, but which could never be mistaken for one of such a group. There is a shade of difference, a unique flavour, about this variation-theme, which is attractive; its pure, soft, staccato chords suggest a woodwind timbre.[1] Its form is *a b b*, each section being eight bars long.

Certain points of interest in the theme, the leaning towards D major at the beginning of part II, and a colourful modification of the chord of the dominant minor thirteenth, reappear in the following four variations. The experiments and novelties of the previous set in Op. 42 are absent in the first three of these, which revert to

[1] The movement has been orchestrated, and very effectively so, by Dr. Hans Gal.

the usual decorated style of former work. Since the theme of the variations is as much a harmonic, or at least a homophonic scheme as a melodic one, there are obvious affinities with the variations in the 'Death and the Maiden' String Quartet. The first three variations contain the same horn-call motives and soft, trumpet-like fanfares of that movement, and also the same preservation of the general structure of the theme, while melodically showing great freedom. Var. III contains a canon between treble and tenor, that is, between the players' right hands, at a half-bar's interval, which is satisfying to play and to hear. It has a Bach-like, *courante* style.

But the crown of the work, the section which raises it above all its contemporary work in the medium, is the fourth, and final, variation, *un poco più lento*. Schubert wrote nothing else like this variation; the key changes to the tonic major and the music is ethereal, remote, full of a lovely, expansive, melodic flowering that calls for exquisite playing. He asks for pianissimo tone (and in one place uses the direction–not very common with him—*ppp*) and above the rich B major harmonies the flute-like, pastoral phrases rise and fall in one streaming song. The music is warm, but passionless; here is, in truth, the 'child-like' Schubert, in the best sense of the word.

A new departure marks the close of the work, that is, a reprise of the opening bars of the theme, marked pianissimo. In this way the work is satisfyingly rounded off and Schubert can adopt his favourite plan of concluding a set of variations with a quiet and sustained coda.

VI

DECLINE: 1827

14. Variations on a theme from Hérold's 'Marie', Op. 82: no. 1.
15. Variations on *Sei mir gegrüsst*, Op. 159.
16. Impromptu in B flat, Op. 142: no. 3.

The last three sets of variations which Schubert composed, and their background, are in complete contrast to those of the previous chapter. The workmanship is inferior; there is almost a reversion to earlier methods, and one feels that his mastery of the form, so hardly won, has weakened. Formal demands have clamped down on him, fettering his imagination and deadening his fire. In the first two, in fact, he seems indifferent as to whether or not the result is worthy of his pen. It is surprising, this, when one considers the power and supremacy of contemporary work—the 'Winterreise' for example, or the two Trios, Op. 99 and Op. 100, whose buoyancy and poetry and depth of feeling overshadow these three pieces, two of which are merely trumpery.

It was not a very happy period for Schubert: bodily aches and ills, financial hardship, and continual failure to achieve an established artistic position, either by operatic success or musical appointment, inevitably cast a gloom. The gloom is not lightened but made more dismal by the brief sunshine of the holiday at Graz in the autumn of 1827.

It is not of much use to seek for external reasons for the inferiority of these three works; if we judge from the choice of themes it is obvious that Schubert felt no strong desire to write any one of them. The choice of a theme from Hérold's opera

80

'Marie' suggests that the variations were mere hackwork. Neither of the other two themes was written for the occasion; one is taken from the opening of a long, elaborate song and worked up into a *bravura* piece for a star violinist, the other derived from an entr'acte in the incidental music to 'Rosamunde'—a theme which he had already used and used again.

The one consolation lies in the fact that the final work, the B flat Impromptu, does something to recapture the old charm and individuality, and is not, like the other two, entirely an artistic failure.

14. VARIATIONS ON A THEME FROM HÉROLD'S 'MARIE', OP. 82:
NO. I.   [D.908]
Pianoforte Duet.   February 1827

On 6 October 1828 the publisher H. A. Probst of Leipzig wrote a letter to Schubert in which these words occur: '. . . Please communicate to me also anything easily understandable *à 4 mains* you may be writing, rather like your variations on the miller's song from 'Marie'. Would not Himmel's theme 'To Alexis'[1] be effectively workable into something of the same kind?' Schubert's set of eight variations on the theme by Hérold had been reviewed with enthusiasm, and at some length, by the Leipzig journal 'Allgemeine Musikalische Zeitung' of 6 February 1828. Among the somewhat pompous terms of approval the only mild objection was to the use of 'modish' chords (presumably the progressions of diminished sevenths, chromatic sevenths, German sixths and augmented seconds in vars. V and VI); the reviewer

---

[1] From Himmel's song-cycle 'Alexis und Ida'. Schumann composed a canon for pianoforte solo on this theme which Probst recommended to Schubert.

stated, moreover, '. . . we declare these variations to be the best of his that have so far come our way.'

Their popularity with the public may be gauged from the fact that the Hamburg firm of Schuberth & Co. re-published them as Op. 82: no. 1, coupling with them the hitherto unknown set in B flat (see p. 38).

It is with something of a shock, then, that we find on reading, or listening to this work, that few things so empty and unrewarding have come from Schubert's pen. It forms a poor conclusion to his series of variations for pianoforte duet, a perfunctory and heartless farewell.

His musical associations with Hérold are not very happy ones, perhaps understandably so when we consider how ill-matched were the two musicians in stature. The pair of extra numbers which Schubert wrote for the Viennese performance of Hérold's 'La Clochette' ('Das Zauberglöckchen') on 20 June 1821, are absurdly out of scale with that light and tuneful work; and the theme which he chose from 'Marie' to serve as a basis for variations is inadequate to a degree.

The impulse to write the set must be due to his attempt to catch the market with a work based on a temporarily popular tune, for the successful performance of 'Marie' in Vienna had just taken place, on 18 December 1826, four months after its première in Paris. It is his only use of the popular operatic number as a basis for variations, and this is surprising when we recall how, in his day, the public craving for such variations was phenomenally indulged by the publishers; moreover he knew of very numerous examples in the work of Mozart and Beethoven. The practice was censured by certain lowering critics during the years that succeeded the outburst, but little of the work produced has survived, or was intended to survive.

The variations were first published by Haslinger, as Op. 82, on 3 September 1827, and dedicated by the composer to a professor of philosophy at Linz, Kajetan Neuhaus. The manuscript became the property of Haslinger's widow, and from her passed eventually to the Prussian State Library.

Hérold's theme has been called inadequate; this is judging it as material for musical variations. It is, in fact, trivial—an embodiment of Gallic frivolity. None the less, of all the numbers in 'Marie', it has the most obvious appeal without being the most acceptable musically. In its place in the opera, as the opening number of Act III, it is undeniably effective. The clack of a water-mill wheel is heard, and the music, by simple devices such as the appogiaturas in the bass, and short, clipped phrases in the upper strings, reproduces the jog-trot sweep of the paddles. It is scored for strings, wood and horns. The song is sung by the miller, Lubin, to the words:

> *Sur la rivière, comme mon père,*
> *Je suis meunier, de mon métier;*
> *J'travaille et chante, l'âme contente,*
> *Car mon moulin m'donne du pain.*
> *De ma boutique, j'ai m'la musique,*
> *Tic tac . . . tique taque . . . etc.*

The libretto was translated for the performance in Vienna by I. F. Castelli (author of Schubert's one-act *Singspiel* 'Die Verschworenen') but other German translations were made later on and have superseded his.

Considered out of its context the miller's song is a plain, diatonic melody offering no distinction of structure or rhythm apart from a certain perkiness in the 'tic tac' phrases. The harmony is Hérold's and the intrusive triplet flourishes were taken up into the theme, by Schubert, from the accompaniment. He was using the melody of another composer's song, and one quite well known to the musical public, and so he makes none of his usual radical alterations. He shortened the closing phrases by a bar or two, altered Hérold's *Allegro* and common-time signature to *Allegretto* and *alla breve*, but the key remains unchanged.

Is it too fanciful to sense a certain awkwardness in this set of variations: to feel that for most of the time Schubert was at a loss what to do, and so fell back on routine treatment without the real drive of his instinct? Externally the variations reveal his usual course of action, by now a familiar one. With no alteration of key, time-signature or form, the first three variations embody the theme in his least interesting 'quick-march' style. The triplet figure becomes more and more prominent and aids in the process of elaboration. Vars. IV and V shift into C minor and A flat respectively, a scheme similar to that of the Octet variation-movement in the same key, but without thereby gaining any new impetus or imaginative drive. The A flat variation, a stereotyped *un poco più lento*, provides another instance of a Schubertian shell with no 'inside'. It should have been comparable to the analogous *Lied*-variations of previous sets, and the style, it is true, resembles in externals, certain song-like episodes in the first movement of the Pianoforte Trio in B flat, Op. 99. Apart from this it is empty of interest. Only towards the close, where there is a 4-bar codetta, do we get a faint warmth of feeling, when the music pauses for a moment before continuing its cold, clattering progress.

The one section of value in these numerous pages is the seventh variation, an *Andantino*, 12/8, in A minor. This provides the only piece of evidence to show that the work is by the Schubert of 1827, the composer on the threshold of 'Winterreise', and it is quite extraordinary, in view of what has gone before, to find in it a hint

of the final song in that cycle—'Der Leiermann': of the drone
bass and the 'hurdy-gurdy' tune:

Ex. 24

But more than that, it is another example of the new developments
hinted at in the slow movement of Op. 42. The first bar is a variant of Hérold's first bar; from then on the section develops this
variant freely and ignores Hérold. It is but seventeen bars long,
and in those few bars Schubert is himself again.

But in var. VIII the empty display, the noise and vulgarity are
resumed, and persist without intermission for nearly as long as the
preceding seven episodes. To quote again from the Leipzig review:

'[The variations should lead] down to a wholly satisfying and
pleasing conclusion, that may be brilliant, or may offer complete
repose....'

We have seen how Schubert, in all his major works in this form,
with the single exception of Op. 35, chose the latter alternative. It
is a fitting commentary on the variations of Op. 82 to point out
that he wrote for them the 'brilliant' ending.

15. *Andantino* FROM THE FANTASY IN C MAJOR: VARIATIONS ON
   Sei mir gegrüsst, OP. 159.   [D.934]

   Pianoforte and violin.   December, 1827

The variations in this Fantasy, based on a favourite song, and
designed for an instrumental soloist, invite comparison with those
based on *Trockne Blumen*, written under similar conditions. It is a
regrettable fact that the same worthless display is found in the one

G   S.V.

as in the other. The decline in quality noticed in the Hérold variations is even more marked in these, which were composed some ten months later.

The soloist for whom Schubert composed the Fantasy was the young Bohemian violinist, Josef Slawjk, and he performed the work, with Karl von Bocklet as pianist, on 20 January 1828. According to the critics, Schubert was better served by his pianist than by his violinist; the work is technically very difficult for both performers, and Slawjk was evidently unable to cope with the virtuoso decoration. The Fantasy, as a whole, found little favour with the audience, many people leaving the hall before the work was concluded. We do find, however, that the critic of the London journal 'Harmonicon' approved of it; his report, printed in July, 1828, stated:

'A new Fantasia for pianoforte and violin from the pen of Franz Schubert possesses merit far above the common order.'
Schubert offered his Fantasy to the publishing firm of B. Schott's Sons in Mainz, but he never despatched it to them, and shortly after his death the manuscript was sold by his brother, Ferdinand, to Diabelli. The latter published it, but not until 1850, as Op. 159. At some time in its career the autograph was torn in two, but both pieces are now in the Vienna City Library.

The variations are based on the song *Sei mir gegrüsst* and constitute the third movement of the work. Unlike the Fantasy for pianoforte solo, Op. 15, this one is not a modified sonata, but very free in form: it resembles the Fantasy in F minor [D.940] (first sketched by Schubert in the following month) as far as externals of structure go, but is very far below it in worth. The first movement is an *Andante Moto*, 6/8, the second an *Allegretto* in A minor, 2/4. After a long preparation on the dominant the set of variations enters in A flat.

As we expect, the theme is changed from that in the song. *Sei mir gegrüsst* was composed in 1822, and published a year later as Op. 20: no. 1. It is the first of Schubert's five magnificent settings of poems by Friedrich Rückert. The ardour and breadth and nobility of the song speak of the greater Schubert. It is constructed on the principle of the rondo—*a b a b a*, the recurrence of *a* and *b* showing powerful and highly emotional modifications each time. The variation-theme takes the exposition of the song—*a b*, and uses a not very imaginative fusion of melody and accompaniment. Thus, in the song, the pianoforte plays a syncopated, accompanying melody whose notes lie a third above those of the voice; in the variation-theme these are fused together so that the true melody of the song is buried in the chords of the pianoforte part. The key of the song, B flat, and the tempo, *langsam*, become in the Fantasy, A flat, and *Andantino*.

The beauty of the song lends its own charm to the announcement of the theme, the first part by the pianoforte alone, the second with the violin added. But there the attraction ends. There are three variations with a short, modulatory coda, and on the whole they form the poorest set that Schubert penned. Even the Hérold variations, even those on *Trockne Blumen*, are not entirely without a passing moment of interest: these are void of any.

The 48 bars of the theme are progressively filled in with scales, in unison, octaves or chords, thick figuration, arpeggios, broken chords, trivial syncopations, ornaments, all without the slightest elevation or distinction; there is merely a bored use of all the tricks of the trade. The second variation reverts to a figure already overworked in the *Allegretto* movement. As each succeeds the other these tricks of filling in the texture gradually curdle the theme, and the accompaniment congeals with the weight of figuration; the music becomes

'. . . like a rich chasuble, so stiff with gold and gems that it stands unsupported, a carapace of jewelled sound, into which the sense, like some snotty little seminarist, irrelevantly creeps and is lost . . .'[1]

For 'sense' read 'melody' or 'meaning' and the description is not far from the truth.

There is a further irritation in that the characteristic cadence of the song, set to the words 'Sei mir geküsst, sei mir gegrüsst', and given in the variation-theme a further sweetening by anticipation:

becomes, on repeated hearing, unbearably wearisome. The genuine emotion of the phrase was *created* in the song: the variations merely exploit it. And the exploitation is a striking confirmation of Dr. R. U. Nelson's sentence in his book 'The Technique of Variation' in which he postulates that

'. . . those elements which are the most conspicuous and hence the most easily and quickly comprehended demand change the most insistently. . . .'

The coda also develops this phrase, and thereby modulates into C major for the finale, *Allegro vivace*. This quick movement is interrupted for a moment by a brief allusion to the theme of the variations, in A flat, marked *Allegretto* (!), and here the composer does show a possibility of serious treatment of the theme; but the episode is only 25 bars long and its purpose is clearly to allow Schubert his favourite shift into a key a third below his tonic key so as to brighten the tonality of the concluding bars when C major returns.

[1] Aldous Huxley: 'Vulgarity in Literature', p. 31.

16. IMPROMPTU IN B FLAT, OP. 142: NO.3.   [D.935]

    Pianoforte Solo.   December 1827

Schubert's eight impromptus for the pianoforte were all written in the autumn of 1827. The first four were called 'Impromptus' by their publisher, Haslinger; Schubert approved the title and adopted it himself for the last four. He offered these, as he had offered the Fantasy for pianoforte and violin, to the Mainz firm of B. Schott's Sons, and indicated to those publishers that they were to form his Op. 101. Nothing came of this offer. The four impromptus were issued posthumously by Diabelli, in 1838, as Op. 142, and dedicated to Liszt. On the manuscript, until recently in the music library of Peters in Leipzig, the pieces are numbered 5 to 8.

The third number of Op. 142, Schubert's seventh impromptu, is a set of variations, and is, perhaps, the most celebrated of the whole series of eight pieces. It is a happy chance that in this work, his last example of variation-form, we find a return to the more personal, more impulsive style of earlier work. He does not say the last word with the bombast and flourish of the two preceding sets, but with his own characteristic voice and accent. Not that the Impromptu possesses any musical value as high as we find in the work of 1824–1826. It offers a modest alternation of lyrical and sentimental verses, of Viennese light-heartedness and Viennese 'Sehnsucht'; Schubert was not often so completely of his own *Biedermeier* period as he is in this work, not so often, in fact, as commentators would have us think. But it is far and away more worthy of his pen than the other variations of that year.

The theme, in its opening bars, closely resembles that of the 'Rosamunde' entr'acte in B flat: a theme which Schubert had re-used in the slow movement of the String Quartet in A minor, and again, in allusive style, in the song *Wiegenlied* to words by Johann

Gabriel Seidl [D.867]. It is perhaps worth pointing out, as an example of Schubert's indifference to such points of detail, that the 'Rosamunde' theme is, in the entr'acte, in 2/4 time, but in the string quartet movement the bars are simply paired off so that the theme appears in 2/2 time; the keys are respectively B flat major and C major. The Impromptu returns to the key of the entr'acte but retains the time-signature of the quartet movement. The short middle section achieves a freshness with its G minor harmonies, although there is little melodic change.

The five variations are not uninfluenced by the experiments of 1825, and all of them, even though in length and general outline they follow the lead of the theme, show great freedom in the treatment of it. This is particularly noticeable in the lilt and flow of var. I, which uses the 'arpeggio' device first found in the keyboard works of 1817, and in the noble, Brahmsian hymn of var. III, which might almost have come from that master's 'Handel' variations of his Op. 24. The freedom of treatment is most marked in the fourth variation of the set, a passage in G flat major, which develops its own initial phrase with only the barest of nods to the theme of its origin. It is difficult in both these variations, nos. IV and V, for the pianist to make their full effect.

A remarkable feature of this Impromptu, and one which, though it cannot escape notice, must obviously have been unintentional on the composer's part, is that it contains several reminiscences of his past work, both of technique and substance. Writing of 'A Winter's Tale', Quiller-Couch describes a tapestried gallery, or a garden, at the close of day, haunted by footfalls, whispers, shadows, that tempt one to say 'I have been here—just here—before, either in this life, or a previous one'. So it is with Schubert's B flat Impromptu. He, of course, could not have been aware that he was writing his last word on the subject; nevertheless, these small details of reference give a strange, valedictory quality to the work.

There is, in the first place, the choice of a theme which is so pregnant with associations of the past; there is, in the penultimate bar of the first part of the theme, the use of the diminished seventh with the E natural in the bass, which recalls a similar penultimate bar in the 'Death and the Maiden' theme of the D minor String Quartet; there is in the fourth variation much that reminds us of the *Andante* movement of the 'Trout' Quintet; there is the return to a feature of his early pianoforte style—the muscular bass runs in the left-hand part; there is the renewed use of those repeated chords with moving parts which were a noteworthy feature of the 'Ten Variations in F major' and of the variations in the Sonata in A minor. We find, again, Schubert repeating the practice, abandoned for many years, of the 'variation-pair': this is most effectively done between vars. II and V:

Finally, there is another use in the coda of a device which was first found in the *Andantino varié*—the bringing back of the theme to form a soft and tranquil close to the whole work. In this Impromptu the 'Rosamunde' theme is given at the end in full chords which contain piquant harmonic changes and delayed resolutions, colourful but subdued, and which form an excellent foil to the sparkling runs of the last variation.

The pianistic style of the work is chiefly admirable—nothing could be more eminently satisfying from a physical standpoint than the first variation. But in the middle of the work we are faced with qualities which are endemic in his keyboard technique, the implications of which cannot be baulked. There is no doubt that Schubert demands of the player, here and elsewhere in his pianoforte works, more than he can adequately perform. Without approaching the manipulative and virtuoso requirements of the great pianist composers, he yet weaves a many-stranded keyboard fabric, in which the fingers simply cannot deal effectively with all that is required of them. It is this reason, without doubt, that led to the rejection of the four impromptus by Schott's Sons, on the grounds that they were too difficult. The only advice to give the performer is that he guard against the attempt to shape a 'broad outline' of the work, at the expense of these points of detail. In Schubert, it is the detail which calls for attention and not the architectural mass.

Before leaving this third number of Op. 142, it may be worth digressing a little in order to consider a matter which concerns the whole opus. It consists of:

    i. *Allegro moderato* in F minor,
    ii. *Allegretto* (with Trio) in A flat,
    iii. Theme and variations in B flat,
    iv. *Allegro scherzando* in F minor.

When this collection of four pieces first appeared, Schumann, enthusiastic but ill-informed, pronounced it to be a dismembered sonata. There have been other scholars, who should know more of the facts than Schumann, who have supported this absurd judgement. We can ignore, perhaps, the fact that Schubert himself called the pieces 'Impromptus' and so wrote of them to publishers; he might have thought that under such a guise there would

be a readier sale. We might possibly overlook the extremely unlikely position of the 'Scherzo' as a second movement, an order
which Schubert never used in a sonata which he himself submitted
for publication. We might even reconcile ourselves to the un-
precedented key-scheme of the work. But the insurmountable
obstacle is the fact that the first Impromptu—which would constitute the first movement if the work had been originally a sonata
—is not in sonata-form: it is a *rondo*. If there is one thing on which
we can take our stand with absolute certainty, it is that Schubert
would never have written a sonata in which the first movement
was not in orthodox sonata-form. This fact alone gives the lie to
any assertion that this opus was originally written as a sonata. In
fact the only point in favour of the theory is the very slight one
that the first and last movements are both in the same key of F
minor; that the first one is neither a 'sonata-form' movement nor,
for all its attraction, in Schubert's 'grand-style' (as are all other
first movements of his, whatever their period or quality) and that
the last piece—a *scherzando*—is a most implausible Schubertian
finale: these considerations are quite overlooked.

APPENDIX

I

The single variation for pianoforte solo, in C minor [D.718], which Schubert wrote on a waltz by the publisher, Anton Diabelli, was composed in March, 1821. It was published on 9 June 1824 as the thirty-eighth of fifty variations, each of which had been contributed by different composers—most of them Austrians, all of them resident at some time in Austria—on Diabelli's invitation. Beethoven's celebrated '33 Variations' on the theme formed Part I of the collection, entitled by Diabelli 'Vaterländischer Künstlerverein'; the other fifty formed Part II. Names which strike one in this huge assembly are those of Liszt (then only a boy of eleven), Moscheles and Czerny, and, in the Schubertian circle, of Anselm Hüttenbrenner and Bocklet.

Diabelli's animated waltz, no worse than thousands of contemporary examples, is sufficiently interesting to provide a variation subject, and sufficiently devoid of conspicuous features to serve admirably the indulgence of sundry variation techniques. Schubert's variation is by no means a negligible page. He preserved the cadential structure of the theme, and used a charming derivative from the bass of the waltz to serve for his melody:

Ex. 27

Although there is no tempo indication the *Vivace* of the original is surely too fast. In style the variation resembles the third movements of his 1817 sonatas for the pianoforte, *cf.* the Scherzo of Sonata no. 6, in E minor, and is not unlike the first waltz of his own Op. 9, which was possibly composed just over a year previously.

The simple chromatic sequences in the waltz are transmuted by the Schubertian touch, and that in the first half, together with its later modification, are examples of the delicate but vivid imagery which is so typical of his pianoforte writing during that period.

It has been suggested by Gerald Abraham that the piece might be given an occasional airing by pianists as a kind of epilogue, or encore, to a performance of the '33 Variations' on the Diabelli theme by Beethoven.

II

Three sets of variations by Schubert are unpublished.

(*a*) There is a set of seven variations in F major [D.24], belonging to his early years, possibly to 1811. The manuscript of these variations was last heard of in 1923; from it a double sheet, containing the end of no. 3, the whole of nos. 4 and 5, and the start of no. 6, is missing.

(*b*) There is an early set of six variations, in E flat [D.21], which was catalogued by his brother, Ferdinand, as belonging to 1812. Ferdinand stated, moreover, that this was the work which the boy Schubert played to his father as the first evidence of his skill as a composer. Kreissle names it '*Andante* and variations'. The work is lost.

(*c*) The third unpublished set [D.597a] is a curiosity. The manuscript, now lost, was said to consist of sketched variations for violin solo. Kreissle mentions the manuscript in his lists of unpublished works as being then in the possession of Ferdinand Schubert. Even the key, A major, and the definite date, December, 1817, are given. For its period a composition for solo violin was a rarity, and from Schubert's pen—one is tempted to add—an impossibility. Ferdinand Schubert nowhere mentions the work in his own catalogues, and it seems more than likely that, in Kreissle's description, details of the accompanying instrument or instruments were, by chance, omitted. There is a Rondo in A major for violin solo and strings of this period (June, 1816) which may also have caused confusion.

III

A feature in many of Schubert's sets of dances, which has some bearing on the subject of this book, calls for notice. It is his tendency, possibly subconscious—but if so none the less interesting, to use variation technique in the progression of a collection of dances, and so to achieve an artistic unity which elevates the collections above their merely transient, social function. This was first pointed out by that excellent Schubertian August Reissmann. In his study of the composer's life and works of 1873 he drew attention to Op. 9, Schubert's first published, but by no means first composed, set of waltzes [D.365]. It is a miscellany of dances; the thirty-six individual items were composed over a period of six years (1816–1821), but from the first dozen or so, which belong to November, 1819, Reissmann quotes the themes of the dances nos. 6, 7(b), 9 and 10(b), and shows clearly that they are variations of the theme in the first dance; the author (in 1873) was unaware of Schubert's actual dates, unaware, that is, that the waltzes were scattered in time, but his interesting conclusions could be used to prove that the first, undated, waltz was of the same month as its associated variants, that is, of November 1819.

The tendency is more marked in dance-sets which have remained as units and have come to us in an undispersed state. As
examples three of these sets may be quoted: 20 minuets of 1813
[D.41]; 5 minuets of November 1813 [D. 89]; 8 Ländler in B flat
of February 1816 [D.378]. The most attractive and striking example of this 'variation-tendency', among others, is in the set of
'8 Ländler in F sharp minor' of 1816 [D.355], which was not
published until Schubert's centenary year, 1928. These are charming dances in themselves, and might have gained a deserved
attention had they been published as a set of 'Ländler-variations'.

IV

Reference may be made to a set of variations closely associated
with Schubert, although not, in fact, his own composition. It
forms the last movement of his so-named 'Guitar' quartet [D.96].
The manuscript of this work, inscribed 'Written in Franz's own
hand' and dated '26 February 1814', was discovered in 1918, and
published in Munich, in 1926, as a hitherto unknown work of
Schubert's, a quartet in five movements for flute, guitar, viola and
cello. Various references on the manuscript, in another's hand, to
a 'Terzetto', led the editor of the published work, Georg Kinsky,
to conclude that Schubert's original conception had been a Trio,
for flute, guitar and viola. O. E. Deutsch's shrewd investigations
into the matter revealed that the work was spurious; it proved to
be an adaptation of a 'Notturno' for flute, guitar and viola by
Wenzel Matiegka, published in 1807 by Artaria & Co. of Vienna
as that composer's Op. 21. The work, strangely enough, was
dedicated to Count Esterházy, Schubert's later employer.

Schubert took Matiegka's 'Trio' and arranged it for flute,
guitar, viola and cello. It is usual to add, in this connection, that he
merely added a cello part and that he did so, probably, for his

father. Two comments must be made here: certain parts of the work, for instance the opening of the third movement, *Lento e patetico*, suggest that the adaptation was more radical than that involved by the simple addition of a cello part; and that the difficulty of the added music would rule out the probability that it was composed by Schubert for his father. Franz Schubert, senior, was a modest performer, and his son's early String Quartets have accommodatingly easy cello parts. Since the manuscript of Schubert's arrangement was found in the possession of the descendants of one Ignaz Rosner, a friend of Schubert's and a cellist, it seems more likely that the quartet version was made for him. The 'Trio no. 2' of the 'Menuetto' (2nd movement) is entirely Schubert's own work.

Considering this mild production of Matiegka's, one wonders how it could ever have been accepted and performed as a work of Schubert, even an early one. There is no single touch throughout which proclaims the young composer's genius; it is modest music, well-written and dull. By February 1814 Schubert had shown what he could produce in the way of instrumental works in the String Quartet in E flat (Op. 125: no. 1) and in the Symphony no. 1, in D. This fact, even in the absence of external evidence, together with the use of the guitar, the presence of a 'Zingara' movement, and, above all, the position, and theme, of the variations, should have raised such doubts as to cause any responsible scholar to withhold recognition of the work as authentically Schubert's. For the variation-movement, in the first place, constitutes the *finale* of the work, and, in the second, it is based upon another composer's song. Both factors are without precedent or sequel in Schubert's work in sonata-form.

The song (G major, 6/8) is a 'Serenade' by Friedrich Fleischmann, 'Do not slumber yet, O Maiden', composed in the year before Schubert's birth. It resembles slightly the 'Cradle-song' of Bernhard Flies which, in like manner, preserves the composer's name by spuriously attaching itself to Mozart.

The three extant variations, nos. II, IV and V, the last of which was incomplete, and furnished with a conclusion by the editor of the publication, in 1926, are trifling and bear no comparison with Schubert's own early work in variation-form. To the first one, in which Matiegka reproduces the melody unchanged, Schubert adds a bass of rioting demisemiquavers. The second is a hymn-like variant of the melody with stolid part-writing, in which the cello part doubles, on octave below, various fragments selected from the guitar and viola parts. The third variation is of the 'figured' type, breaking the melody up into repeated chords and florid runs, with quite effective *pizzicato* interludes for viola and cello.

It is a singular thing that this misattribution of Matiegka's 'Notturno' has rescued his name from complete oblivion; it is not given a line in any standard work of reference. One is reminded of similar examples: in the case of August von Weyrauch, who is accorded remembrance solely because a song of his, *Adieu*, was also once misattributed to Schubert, and in the case of Anton Fischer, whose comic Trio, *Die Advokaten*, was published as Schubert's Op. 74, and which fact confers on him, too, a vicarious renown.

INDEX OF SCHUBERT'S WORKS

Titles of songs and operas in Italics

GENERAL INDEX

Abraham, Gerald, 95
'Allgemeine Musikalische Zeitung' (Vienna), 50
'Allegemeine Musikanzeiger' (Frankfurt), 73
'Allgemeine Musikzeitung' (Leipzig), 73, 81, 85
Artaria & Co. (Vienna), 97

Bach, 4, 10, 69, 70, 79
    Chaconne in D minor (violin solo), 10
    'Goldberg' Variations, 4
    Mass in B minor ('Crucifixus'), 70
    'Wohltemperirtes Klavier' Fugues, 69
Barth, Josef, 42, 62
Basso ostinato, 4
Baumberg, Gabriele von, 25
Beethoven, 2, 5, 6, 9, 10, 11, 12, 14, 15, 16, 17, 28, 33, 34, 82
    'Allegretto' from Symphony no. 7, 29, 54, 69, 70
    Diabelli 'Waltz' (33 variations on), 12, 94, 95
    'Kreutzer' Sonata, Op. 47, 2
    Septet, Op. 20, 58
    Sonata in E, Op. 109, 14
    String Quartet in E flat, Op. 127, 12
Beethoven, Karl von, 34
Berchtold, Count Anton, 68
Bocklet, Karl von, 86, 94
Bogner, Ferdinand, 42, 53
'Bon Chevalier, Le', 32
Brahms, 10, 12
    'Handel' Variations, Op. 24, 90
Breitkopf & Haertel (Leipzig), 21
Bruckner, Anton, 9
Buxtehude, Dietrich, 3
Byrd, William, 3

Capell, Richard, 9, 23, 48
Cappi & Diabelli (Vienna), 50, 60
Castelli, Ignaz Franz, 83
Congress of Vienna, 17
Conservatoire de Paris, 24
Couperin, François, 4
Czerny, Josef (Vienna), 45, 62
Czerny, Karl, 1, 9, 94

Delius, Frederick, 12
Deutsch, Otto Erich, 8, 33, 68, 69, 97
Diabelli, Anton, 94
Diabelli & Co. (Vienna), 24, 30, 33, 44, 86, 89
Dresel, Otto, 33
Drouet, Louis, 33, 35
'Egmont' (Goethe), 23
Einstein, Alfred, 3
Elgar, Sir Edward, 13
    'Enigma' Variations, 13
Esterházy family, 33, 67
Esterházy, Count Johann, 32, 97
Esterházy, Karoline, 32, 38, 69
Esterházy, Marie, 32, 38, 69

Farnaby, Giles, 3
Fleischmann, Friedrich, 98
Flies, Bernard, 99
Franck, César, 12
Friedlaender, Max, 48
Fröhlich, Barbara, 53

Gahy, Josef von, 35
Gal, Hans, 43, 78
'Gesellschaft der Musikfreunde' (Vienna), 21
Glock, William, 40
Goethe, 23, 77
Grove, Sir George, 72
Gymnich, August von, 43

'Harmonicon' (London), 86
Haslinger, Tobias (Vienna), 38, 83, 89
Haydn, 4, 9, 15, 17, 42, 73
    'Emperor' String Quartet, 42
    Variations in F minor, 4
Hérold, Louis, 12, 17, 38, 80, 82, 83, 84, 85
    'La Clochette', 82
    'Marie', 81, 82, 83
Himmel, Friedrich, 81
Horni, —, 49
Hortense, Queen of Holland, 32
Hummel, Johann, 9, 50
    Piantoforte Quintet, Op. 87, 45